new
business
card
GRAPHICS
2

P·I·E BOOKS

P·I·E BOOKS

Villa Phoenix Suite 301, 4-14-6, Komagome,
Toshima-ku, Tokyo 170-0003 Japan
Tel: 03-3940-8302 Fax: 03-3576-7361
e-mail: editor@piebooks.com
         sales@piebooks.com

ISBN 4-89444-117-9 C3070

Printed in Japan

EDITORIAL NOTES

credit format

CLIENT
Country of Client

creative staff

cd: creative director
ad: art director
 d: designer
 p: photographer
 i: illustrator
cw: copywriter
df: design Firm

TYPE OF BUSINESS

Please note that some credit data has been omitted at the request of the submittor.

※The labelling of card faces as "front" and "back" was based on our editorial judgement.

Small, easy-to-transport, occupy little storage space, yet display the required information; what media could be so simple and convenient? — business cards. Compared to catalogs or posters they are relatively easy to produce, hence many people create them not only for business, but for private use as well. We tend to think of this being a fairly recent trend, but a tale of America's frontier days includes an episode in which young girls order and exchange calling cards. They are shown in a small-town printing shop deliberating over what typeface and motif to use, and later, handing out their precious cards sparingly only to their very best friends. Interestingly, business cards were already understood as a vehicle for expressing one's identity symbolically by the average person even back in those days.

Back to the book at hand . . . this volume introduces 850 business cards from countries around the world having one essential thing in common a strong sense of presence. The previous volume revealed a distinct split: cards from the design and retail worlds were more idiosyncratic, while cards from the business world tended to be somewhat stiff. That generalization, however, is recently no longer applicable. Perhaps this stems from the fact that businesses too are now creating business cards that support a distinctive identity. Consequently, we dispensed with categorizing by the cards by type of business for this volume, grouping them instead, for easy reference, by design approach as:

Minimal & Formal : *orthodox and refined in design*
Hyper & Leading Edge : *designs incorporating photography and digital type*
Simple & Chic : *sophisticated and elegant in design*
Pop & Casual : *humorous and flamboyant*

Whichever the category every card is distinctive — the kind you would want to safe if you received it. It is our hope that this volume will serve to stimulate the readers' senses, and to inspire the creation of business cards displaying freer thinking and greater individuality.

Finally, we would like to express our gratitude to all who contributed works and efforts in the production of this book.

P·I·E Books Editorial Staff

Klein, leicht zu transportieren, brauchen wenig Platz—und zeigen doch alle nötigen Informationen; welches Medium kann so simpel und bequem sein? Die Visitenkarte. Verglichen mit Katalogen oder Plakaten sind sie relativ leicht herzustellen. Deswegen produzieren sie viele Leute nicht nur für den Geschäfts-, sondern auch für den Privatgebrauch. Wir meinen, das sei ein ziemlich neuer Trend, aber eine Erzählung aus den Tagen des amerikanischen Wilden Westen erwähnt sie in einer Episode, in der junge Mädchen Visitenkarten bestellen und untereinander austauschen. Die Mädchen diskutieren in einer Kleinstadt-Druckerei darüber, welche Schrift und welche Motive sie benutzen wollen. Später wird beschrieben, wie sie ihre wertvollen Karten sorgsam an ihre besten Freunde verteilen. Interessanterweise wurden bereits damals vom Normalbürger die Visitenkarten als Vehikel verstanden, um die persönliche Identität symbolisch auszudrücken.

Zurück zu diesem Buch. Dieser Band stellt 850 Visitenkarten aus Ländern rund um den Globus vor. Alle haben eine wesentliche Eigenschaft gemein—ihre starke Präsenz. Im ersten Band konnte man eine klar erkennbare Trennung bemerken: Visitenkarten aus der Design- und Einzelhandelswelt waren eher speziell und verrückt, während Karten aus der Business-Welt dazu tendierten, etwas steif zu sein. Diese Verallgemeinerung kann man jetzt nicht mehr machen. Wahrscheinlich stammt dies aus dem Faktum, daß heute jede Art von Firma Visitenkarten haben will, die eine eigene Identität vermitteln. Konsequenterweise haben wir die Kategorisierung jetzt geändert. Wir stellen Ihnen nun zur leichteren Übersicht die Visitenkarten nach Design-Ansatz vor:

Minimal & Formal : *orthodox, pur im Design*
Hyper & Leading Edge : *Design, mit Photografie und digitaler Schrift*
Simple & Chic : *elegant im Design*
Pop & Casual : *humorvoll, aufmerksamkeitsheischend*

In welche Kategorie die Karte auch fällt, hier sind nur Beispiele von Visitenkarten, die man gerne aufheben würde, wenn man sie bekommt. Wir hoffen, daß dieses Buch die Sinne des Lesers anregt und auch zur Gestaltung von Visitenkarten inspiriert, die freieres Denken und größere Individualität erkennen lassen.

Letztendlich möchten wir allen herzlich danken, die mit ihren Arbeiten zu diesem Buch beigetragen haben.

Das Redaktionsteam von P·I·E Books

vorwort

thanks to Paul M. Preiser GmbH in Germany

P·I·E Books wishes to extend

for allowing us to use their products

in our editorial design.

contents

KOICHI SATO (Japan)
AD, D: Koichi Sato *Graphic Designer*

Dr. med. & Dr. phil.

MARIO B. ROBBIANI-FREY

Facharzt FMH *für* GYNÄKOLOGIE & GEBURTSHILFE

Marktgasse 4, 4051 Basel, T 061 261 35 10, F 061 261 35 16

MARIO B. ROBBIANI-FREY (Switzerland)
CD, AD, D: Lucia Frey DF: Wild & Frey *Gynecologist*

front

FLY PRODUCTIONS (USA)
AD, D: Marc Hohmann / Akiko Tsuji DF: Kon/Struktur
Event Production

MELISSA D'ATTILIO
FLY PRODUCTIONS
430 WEST 24TH ST. 6B NEW YORK, NY 10011
TEL: 212 989 3188 FAX: 212 366 1017

back

FLY PRODUCTIONS (USA)

STORM
MARKET LEADING DESIGN
149 FIFTH AVENUE NEW YORK NY 10010
PHONE 212 979 1004 FACSIMILE 212 979 1708
souter@storm-nyla.com
STORM DESIGN LLC NEW YORK LOS ANGELES

STORM DESIGN, LLC (USA)
CD, AD, D: Marc Hohmann DF: Kon/Struktur *Design Firm*

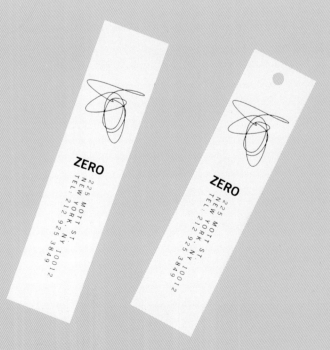

ZERO (USA)
AD, D: Marc Hohmann / Akiko Tsuji DF: Kon/Struktur *Boutique*

1. URSULA WILD (Switzerland) AD, D: Heinz Wild DF: Wild & Frey *Foot-Massage Therapist*
2. DIGITAL PRINT ZURICH AG (Switzerland) CD, AD, D: Lucia Frey / Heinz Wild DF: Wild & Frey *Printer*

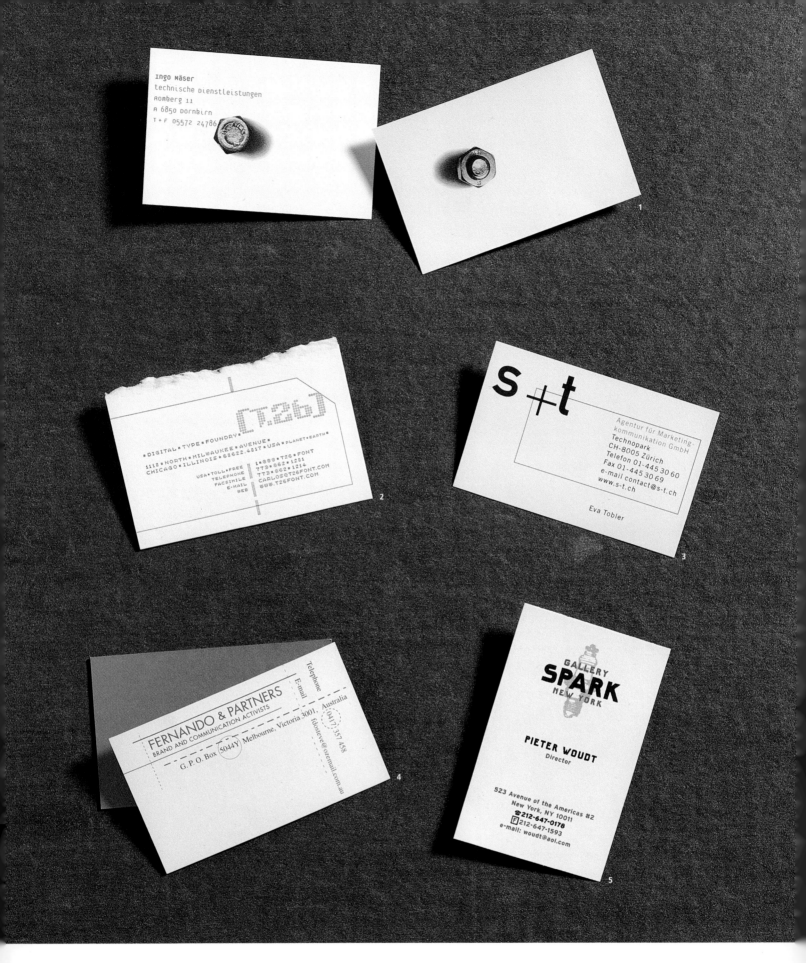

1, INGO MÄSER (Austria) AD, D: Sigi Ramoser *Locksmith*
2, [T-26] (USA) CD, AD, D: Carlos Segura DF: Segura Inc. *Digital Type Foundry*
3, S+T MARKETING COMMUNICATIONS (Switzerland) CD, AD, D: Lucia Frey DF: Wild & Frey *Marketing Communications Company*
4, FERNANDO & PARTNERS (Australia) CD, AD, D: Andrew Hoyne DF: Hoyne Design *Brand & Planning Consultancy*
5, GALLERY SPARK (USA) D: Pieter Woudt DF: Big Bolt Graphics *Gallery*

PASCAL WÜEST (Switzerland) CD, AD, D: Lucia Frey P: Pascal Wüest DF: Wild & Frey *Phtotgrapher*

MOTIVE DESIGN RESEARCH (USA) CD, AD, D, P, I: Denise Heckman DF: Motive Design Research *Design Firm*

SHINICHI AOKI (Japan)
CD, AD, D, Calligrapher: Kenji Ohi DF: Design
Office OO1 *Personal*

（株）増辰海苔店

◆本社
東京都千代田区九段北4-1-9
電話 03-3262-9875
FAX. 03-3262-9878
◆埼玉営業所・工場
埼玉県吉川市栄町1505
電話 0489-82-1627
FAX. 0489-82-1688

http://www.mastaz.com/

海から直送、グルメ特急便。

取締役埼玉営業所長
商品開発室長
増田泰彦

MASUTATSU-NORITEN (Japan)
D: Kennedy Design *Food Manufacturer & Retailer*

（有）平間 至

フォトグラファー
平間 至

東京都渋谷区神宮前2・31・7
ビラ・グロリア403号室【郵便番号】150・0001
電話 03・3405・9196　電送 03・3405・9186

ITARU HIRAMA (Japan)
DF: Tycoon Graphics *Photographer*

二宮 秀介

Monji

CYV00040　niftyid
〇五〇・四八七五五八一　phs
〇九三・七七一・七二六三　tel
郵便番号八〇八・〇〇六四
北九州市若松区宮丸一・二五・五

MONJUAN (Japan)
D: Hiroyuki Matsuishi *Photographer*

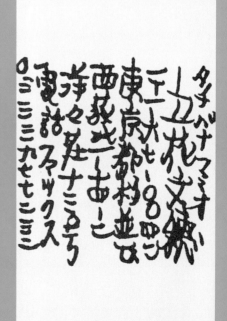

FUMIO TACHIBANA (Japan)
AD, D: Fumio Tachibana
Graphic Designer

ARCHITECTURE & CHILDREN NETWORK (Japan) D: Takaaki Kihara CW: Takeshi Inaba *Non-Profit Oraganization*

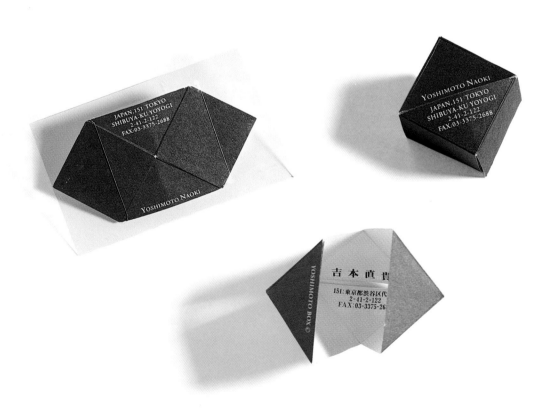

NAOKI YOSHIMOTO (Japan) CD: Naoki Yoshimoto AD, D: Katsunori Aoki *Artist*
※*The body of the card separates from its transparent base and assembles into a dimensional object.*

DO (Netherlands) CD, AD: Erik Kessels CD, CW: Johan Kramer DF: Kesselskramer *Brand in Mentality*

FORK (Japan)
CD, D: Toshihiro Suzuki AD: Ikuo Ueda DF: VIE Inc.
Graphic Design Firm

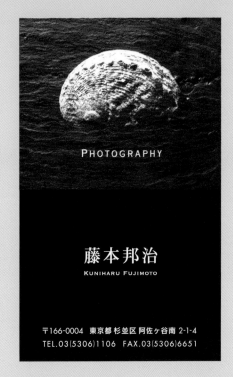

KUNIHARU FUJIMOTO (Japan)
AD, P: Kuniharu Fujimoto D: Yutaka Ichimura
Photographer

SAKAI OSAMU TACTICS ROOM (Japan)
AD, D: Shigeru Kanematsu DF: O-Five Remix
Design Firm

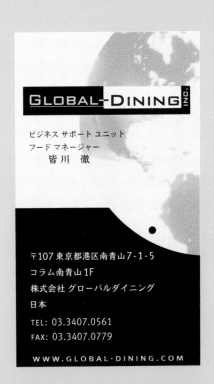

GLOBAL-DINING, INC. (Japan)
CD, AD, D: Petrula Vrontikis DF: Vrontikis Design Office
International Restaurant Group

GLOBAL-DINING, INC. (Japan)
CD, AD, D: Petrula Vrontikis DF: Vrontikis Design Office
International Restaurant Group

1, RON RABIN (USA) CD, AD, D: Rick Eiber P: Ron Rabin DF: Rick Eiber Design (RED) *Photographer*
2, GESINE GROTRIAN (Germany) CD, AD, D: Gesine Grotrian P: Ralf M. Mendle DF: Gesine Grotrian Design *Illustrator & Designer*
3, NICOLE SCHADE (Germany) AD, D: Fons M. Hickmann DF: Fons M. Hickmann Design *Copywriter*

z e f a

zefa visual media gmbh

Jens Haas
Chief Editor

Schanzenstrasse 20
D 40549 Düsseldorf
T +49.211.55 06 79
F +49.211.55 29 38
e-mail jens.haas@zefa.de
www.zefa.de

ZEFA VISUAL MEDIA (Germany)
AD, D: Fons M. Hickmann DF: Fons M. Hickmann
Design *Stock Image Agency*

completo

2-32-8-1201
ikejiri setagaya-ku
tokyo 154

telephone·facsimile
03-3411-6389

art director
takeshi
nishimura

COMPLETO INC. (Japan)
AD, D: Takeshi Nishimura DF: Completo Inc.
Graphic Design Firm

タナセシンジ

GRANDCANYON ENTERTAINMENT INC. (Japan)
CD, AD, D: Shinji Tanase
DF: Grandcanyon Entertainment Inc.
Design Firm

UHLMANN

Germaine Uhlmann

Uhlmann Werbeagentur
Merkurstrasse 9
8953 Dietikon
Telefon 01 745 90 45
Telefax 01 745 90 46

UHLMANN (Switzerland)
CD, AD, D: Lucia Frey DF: Wild & Frey
Advertising Agency

DAVIES

118 Berkeley Street
Toronto, Ontario
M5A 2W9
Fax 416 367-8778

Ken Davies Photography 416 367-3223

KEN DAVIES PHOTOGRAPHY (Canada)
CD, AD, D: Roslyn Eskind D: Heike Sillaste
DF: Roslyn Eskind Associates Limited
Photographer

friseur
quellenstrasse 1
6900 bregenz
di - fr 9.00 - 20.00 sa 9.00 - 13.00
tel 05574 529 09

hans berkmann

4·14·32·903 SEKIMACHI-MINAMI
NERIMA-KU, TOKYO 177 JAPAN

TEL/FAX 03·3929·6373

WITZGALL FRISEUR (Austria)
AD, D: Sigi Ramoser DF: Atelier für Text und Gestaltung *Hairdresser*

Isabella Cechowicz

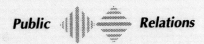

Public **Relations**

Tel. 0241/38429
Hubertusstr. 63, D-52064 Aachen

KAY WAKABAYASHI GRAPHIC DESIGN (Japan)
AD, D: Kay Wakabayashi DF: Kay
Wakabayashi Graphic Design
Graphic Design Firm

ISABELLA CECHOWICZ (Germany)
CD, AD, D: Tadeusz Piechura CW: Isabella Cechowicz
DF: Atelier Tadeusz Piechura *Public Relations*

TANTERI
& ASSOCIATES, INC.

Lighting
Consultants

Matthew C. Tanteri
IES, IALD

The Soho Building
110 Greene Street, Suite 409, NY, NY 10012
Tel: 212. 925. 8265 Fax: 212. 925. 8268

Michiel de Cleen

tandarts
Schubertstraat 40-I
1077 GV AMSTERDAM
020-761945
privé
Prinsengracht 193-B
1015 DS AMSTERDAM
020-241193

TANTERI & ASSOC. (USA)
CD, AD, D, I: Mike Quon DF: Mike Quon / Designation Inc.
Lighting Consultants

MICHIEL DE CLEEN (Netherlands)
D: Pieter Woudt DF: Big Bolt Graphics
Dentist

back

Ralf M Mendle

Alpenerstrasse 11   T 0221.95 53 34.7   M 0172.29 67 317
50825 Köln   F 0221.95 53 34.8   mendle@netcologne.de

front

RALF M. MENDLE (Germany)

RALF M. MENDLE (Germany) CD, AD, D: Gesine Grotrian DF: Gesine Grotrian
Design *Photographer*

< ALEX KOEK
PROJECT EXECUTIVE

PEN & MOUSE
ASSOCIATES

200 JALAN SULTAN TEXTILE CENTRE #25-1Í SINGAPORE 199018

front

PEN & MOUSE ASSOCIATES (Singapore)
CD, AD, D: Michael Koek AD, D: Tjiam Joe Kok
DF: Pen & Mouse Associates *Design Firm*

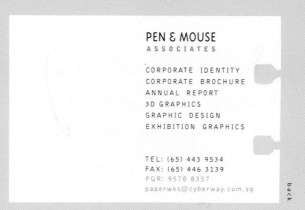

PEN & MOUSE
ASSOCIATES

CORPORATE IDENTITY
CORPORATE BROCHURE
ANNUAL REPORT
3D GRAPHICS
GRAPHIC DESIGN
EXHIBITION GRAPHICS

TEL: (65) 443 9534
FAX: (65) 446 3139
PGR: 9578 8357
paperwks@cyberway.com.sg

back

PEN & MOUSE ASSOCIATES (Singapore)

THE BLUE ROCK
EDITING COMPANY

=DAVID=ROSEN=
=EXECUTIVE=VICE=PRESIDENT=
=AND=GENERAL=COUNSEL=

BLUE ROCK (USA)
CD, AD, D: Carlos Segura DF: Segura Inc. *Editing Company*

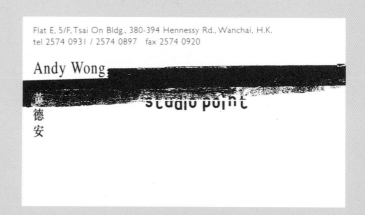

Flat E, 5/F, Tsai On Bldg., 380-394 Hennessy Rd., Wanchai, H.K.
tel 2574 0931 / 2574 0897   fax 2574 0920

Andy Wong

黃
德   studio point
安

STUDIO POINT (Hong Kong) CD, AD, D, I: James Wai Mo Leung
DF: Genesis Advertising Co *Photography Studio*

Mieke Eberhardt
Ideal, Clou, Schloss 1 und 2
Kasinostr. 13, 5000 Aarau
T 064 22 48 82 F 24 29 71

Mieke Eberhardt
Ideal, Clou, Schloss 1 und 2
Kasinostr. 13, 5000 Aarau
T 064 22 48 82 F 24 29 71

KINOS AARAU (Switzerland)
CD, AD: Heinz Wild D: Marietta Albinus DF: Wild & Frey
Movie Theater

242 W 38TH ST NEW YORK NY 10018 PHONE 212 704 4038 FAX 704 0651

ANNI KUAN

ANNI KUAN DESIGN (USA)
CD, AD: Stefan Sagmeister D: Hjalti Karlsson DF:Sagmeister Inc.
Fashion Designer

HISAZUMI DESIGN ROOM (Japan)
AD: Yoshinari Hisazumi D: Tetsuya Hoshiya DF: Hisazumi Design Room
Graphic Design Firm

JOSTMEYER (Netherlands)
CD, AD, D: Annebeth Nies D: Rob Stahl
DF: Stahl Design *Eyewear Retailer*

SUWARY S. A. (Poland)
CD, AD, D: Tadeusz Piechura CW: Henryk Owczarek DF: Atelier
Tadeusz Piechura *Plastic Packaging Manufacturer*

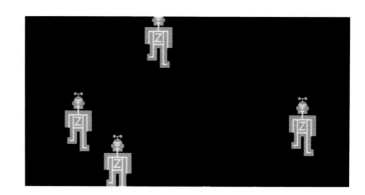

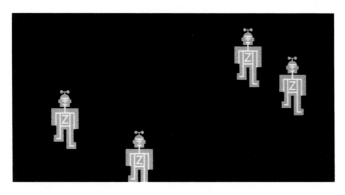

zilliant

Austin, Texas
www.zilliant.com
512.347.3293
pzandan@zilliant.com

Peter Zandan, Ph.D.

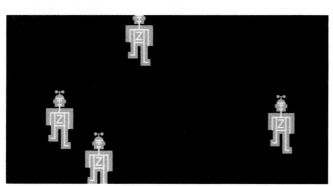
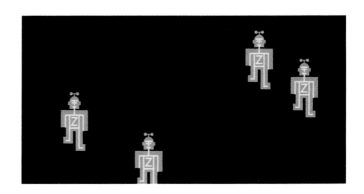

ZILLIANT (USA) CD, AD, D: Matt Heck AD, I: Rex Peteet D: Ty Taylor DF: Sibley/Peteet Design *Internet Researcher*

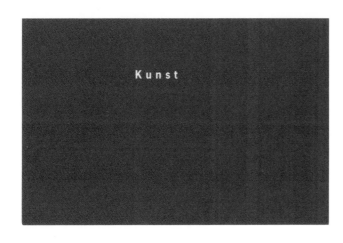

Marion Kotula Studer
Kunsthistorikerin

Kaspar-Schoch-Straße 1
6900 Bregenz Austria
T F ++43 (0) 5574 53449 .

MARION STUDER KOTULA (Austia) AD, D: Sigi Ramoser *Art Historian*

GARDENS (USA) CD, AD, D, I: Mark Brinkman CD, AD, D: Matt Heck DF: Sibley/Peteet Design *Home & Garden Goods Supplier*

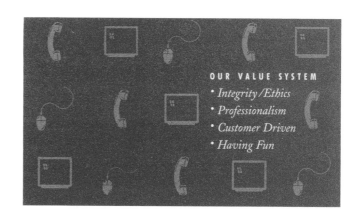

CLEARSOURCE (USA) CD, AD, D, I: Rex Peteet D, I: Carrie Eko DF: Sibley/Peteet Design *Communication Company*

TV Radio Print Multimedia

D4 Creative Group

4100 Main Street, Suite 210
Philadelphia, PA 19127-1623

215.483.4555 phone
215.483.4554 fax
lee@d4creative.com email
www.d4creative.com

Wicky Lee
Senior Art Director

front

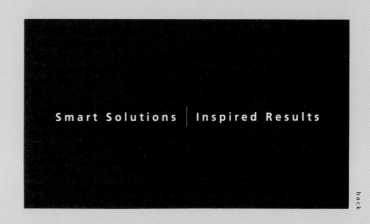
Smart Solutions | Inspired Results

back

D4 CREATIVE GROUP (USA)
AD, I: Wicky W. Lee CW: Paul Fitzgerald
DF: D4 Creative Group *Advertising Agency*

D4 CREATIVE GROUP (USA)

Thomas Grusch

A-1090 Vienna | Pelikangasse 4/25 | fonfax: ++43 [1] 403 46 53 | e-mail: grusch@netway.at

JAMES H. KRAMER VICE PRESIDENT, SALES & CUSTOMER SERVICE

FIRSTWORLD NETWORK
SPECTRANET INTERNATIONAL

201 S. ANAHEIM BLVD, STE 501 ANAHEIM, CALIFORNIA 92805
TELEPHONE (714) 254 4100 FACSIMILE (714) 518 4639
PAGER (800) 463 8556 EMAIL JKRAMER@FIRSTWORLD.COM

THOMAS GRUSCH (Austria)
CD: Thomas Koch DF: The Lounge *Light Designer*

FIRSTWORLD COMMUNICATIONS (USA)
CD, AD, D: John Ball D: Kathy Carpentier-Moore DF: Mires Design, Inc.
Phone & Data Network Company

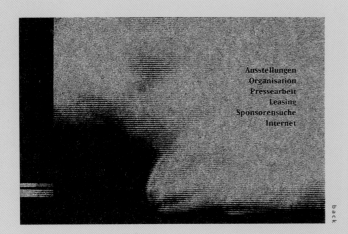
Ausstellungen
Organisation
Pressearbeit
Leasing
Sponsorensuche
Internet

back

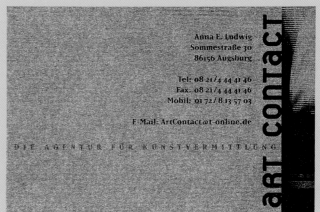
Anna E. Ludwig
Sommestraße 30
86156 Augsburg

Tel: 08 21/4 44 41 46
Fax: 08 21/4 44 41 46
Mobil: 01 72/8 13 57 03

E-Mail: ArtContact@t-online.de

DIE AGENTUR FÜR KUNSTVERMITTLUNG

art contact

front

ART CONTACT (Germany)
CD, AD, D, P, CW: Ilja Sallace DF: Pilot Design Agentur *Art Agency*

ART CONTACT (Germany)

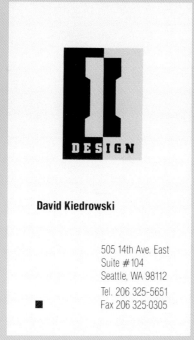

〒150-0046 東京都渋谷区松涛2-21-3

fax + 81-3-5790-0012

saru@saru.co.jp

2-21-3 Shoutou, Shibuya-ku, Tokyo, Japan.

サルブルネイ
SaruBRUNEI

David Kiedrowski

505 14th Ave. East
Suite #104
Seattle, WA 98112
Tel. 206 325-5651
Fax 206 325-0305

SARU BRUNEI, CO., LTD. (Japan)
D: Gento Matsumoto DF: Saru BRUNEI, Co., Ltd.
Design Firm

STAHL DESIGN (Netherlands)
CD, AD, D: Annebeth Nies / Rob Stahl DF:
Stahl Design *Graphic Design Firm*

I DESIGN (USA)
CD, D: Greg Walters DF: Greg Walters Design
Exhibit Design Firm

※*Scratch-card printing reveals a different staff member's name
under different portions of the card.*

〒150-0046 東京都渋谷区松涛2-21-3

fax + 81-3-5790-0012

saru@saru.co.jp

2-21-3 Shoutou, Shibuya-ku, Tokyo, Japan.

サルブルネイ
SaruBRUNEI

67a

koning clovisstraat

6226 ag maastricht

t 043 363 35 77

f 043 362 66 67

rob stahl

[ntwrpr]

SARU BRUNEI, CO., LTD. (Japan)

STAHL DESIGN (Netherlands)

I DESIGN (USA)

CELSIUS FILMS INCORPORATED.

37 east 18th street
new york, new york. 10003 usa

212.253.7400 (t) 212.253.8199 (f)

CELSIUS FILMS (USA)
CD, AD, D, I: Carlos Segura DF: Segura Inc. *Film Production*

CELSIUS FILMS (USA)

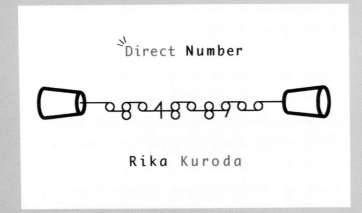

RIKA KURODA (Japan)
D: Takashi Kuroda DF: Kuroda Design Office *Graphic Designer*

RIKA KURODA (Japan)
D: Takashi Kuroda DF: Kuroda Design Office *Graphic Designer*

DOKTOR
REINOLD
BÖHLER

arzt für allgemeinmedizin
6850 dornbirn
mitteldorfgasse 4
t 05572 52630
f 05572 52630-11

DOKTOR BÖHLER (Austria)
D: Sigi Ramoser / Klaus Österle DF: Atelier für Text und Gestaltung *Doctor*

DOKTOR BÖHLER (Austria)

Writer

久保加緒里

〒156-0052
東京都世田谷区
経堂 2-33-5
Phone & Fax.
03-3425-6128
DoCoMo.
020-56-02047

Writer

Kaori Kubo

2-33-5
Kyodo, Setagaya-ku,
Tokyo 156-0052, Japan.
Phone & Fax.
03-3425-6128
DoCoMo.
020-56-02047

KAORI KUBO (Japan)

KAORI KUBO (Japan)
AD: Yoshinari Hisazumi D: Tetsuya Hoshiya DF: Hisazumi Design Room *Writer*

MITSUI
DENTAL
CLINIC

歯学博士
三井安治

医療法人社団 三井歯科クリニック

104 東京都中央区築地 6-4-9 大長ビル2F
Tel & Fax (03) 3541-7186

MITSUI DENTAL CLINIC (Japan)
CD: Akiko Iisaka AD, D: Akihiko Tsukamoto *Dental Clinic*

6-28-14, Daita, Setagaya-ku, Tokyo | 155-0033 Japan.

Tel/03-3469-8550 Fax/03-3469-8567
Handy/030-22-60932

Photographer ■ **Hirohiko Mochizuki**

+M
Hirohiko Mochizuki

HIROHIKO MOCHIZUKI (Japan)
AD: Yoshinari Hisazumi D: Tetsuya Hoshiya DF: Hisazumi Design Room
Photographer

SOSU (Japan)

ソスウ

SOSU
MIHARAYASUHIRO

〒107-0062 東京都港区南青山
5-3-5 ミル・ロッシュビル B1
tel.&fax. 03・3499・9281
Mille Roches build. B1
5-3-5, Minamiaoyama,
Minato-ku, Tokyo, Japan

SOSU (Japan)
AD: Eiki Hidaka D: Ryosuke Uehara DF: Draft Co., Ltd. *Shoes Retailer*

FOUNTAINHEAD (USA)
D: Pieter Woudt DF: Big Bolt Graphics *Video Production*

JACKSON SPORTS MANAGEMENT (USA)
CD, AD: Stan Evenson D: Emma Whipple DF: Evenson Design Group
Sports Management Company

UNIF/X (USA)
D: Pieter Woudt DF: Big Bolt Graphics *Computer Programming Company*

READING ENTERTAINMENT (USA)
CD, AD: Stan Evenson D: Mark Sojka DF: Evenson Design Group
Entertainment Production Company

WELLS FARGO INNOVISIONS (USA) AD, D: Jack Anderson D: Kathy Saito / Alan Copeland DF: Hornall Anderson Design Works, Inc. *ATM Distributor*

CANN (Japan) DF: K's Project Co., Ltd. *Stylist*

346 North Vermont Avenue # 405
Los Angeles, CA 90004, USA
tel./fax 213 / 913 2229
e-mail motionpi@earthlink.net

MOTION PICTURE

DENNIS CHOW   TOP STYLIST

SHOP 2 GROUND FLOOR SINO PLAZA   255-257 GLOUCESTER ROAD   CAUSEWAY BAY H.K.
TEL: **2895 3800   2895 2998**   OPENING HOURS: 10:00 A.M. TO 7:30 P.M. DAILY

MARCIN T. PIECHURA (Poland)
CD, AD, D: Tadeusz Piechura CW: Marcin T. Piechura DF: Atelier Tadeusz Piechura
Motion Pictures Company

JUN FOR HAIR (Hong Kong)
AD, D: Iris Kwok Typeface Designer: Gabriel Tsang DF: Tupos Design Company
Beauty Salon

Kym Little
Marketing Manager

Tel: 03 9239 8880   92 Carroll Road
Fax: 03 9562 8686   South Oakleigh
Mob: 0411 101 136   VIC 3167 Australia

NOEL FERNANDEZ C.
ADMINISTRATIVO DE DATOS

EXCELENCIA EN SERVICIO

OTRACO

OTRACO CHILE S.A.
LA COMPANIA DEDICADA A
NEUMATICOS MUEVETIERRA

ESCONDIDA SITE
SUCRE 220, OF. 509
CASILLA 1080
ANTOFAGASTA, CHILE
FONO +56-55-203 459
FAX +56-55-261 187
noel.fernandez@otraco.com
http://www.otraco.com

TOMASETTI PAPER HOUSE (Australia)
CD: Mimmo Cozzolino AD, D, I: Darren Ledwich DF: Cozzolino Ellett Design D'Vision
Paper Merchants

OTRACO INTERNATIONAL PTY LTD. (Australia)
CD, D, I: Mike Barker AD: Rick Lambert DF: Rick Lambert Design
Earth Mover Tire Management Firm

HOOKER COCKRAM

Andrew Gilfillan
Grad. Cert. Bldg. Mgt
Site Manager

Hooker Cockram Limited   **Telephone** +61 3 9818 3833
32-34 Burwood Road   **Mobile** 015 535 672
Hawthorn Victoria 3122 Australia **Facsimile** +61 3 9818 7734
Email andgil@hcl.com.au

HORNER
LOGISTICS

Kim Shearn MANAGING DIRECTOR

105-109 Munster Terrace, Nth Melbourne Victoria 3051 Australia
Tel+613 9933 8188   Mob 0418 335 385   Fax+613 9933 8181
E-mail logistics@horner.com.au

HOOKER COCKRAM LIMITED (Australia)
CD, AD: Phil Ellett D: Katharine Burke DF: Cozzolino Ellett Design D'Vision
Design Firm

HORNER LOGISTICS (Australia)
CD, AD, D, I: Phil Ellett DF: Cozzolino Ellett Design D'Vision
Computer Warehouse

trigger publishing
40A Pagoda Street Singapore 059199
(65) 224 4383 tel   (65) 224 9209 fax

Jackson Tan + design
224 3851 dir

back

front

TRIGGER MAGAZINE (Singapore)

TRIGGER MAGAZINE (Singapore)
D: Jackson Tan / William Chan / Alvin Tan / Melvin Chee / Perry Neo DF: Trigger
Publisher

web development
corporate identity
print work
multimedia
online strategy

film/video
production

Miami_New York

back

productions interactive

DAVID LOREN CLARKE
dlc@burnww.net

3701 NE 2nd Ave.
Studio "C"
Miami, FL 33137
t 305 438 1800
f 305 438 1560

300 Mercer St.
Suite 9k
New York, NY 10003
212 353 9876tel
212 375 1581fax

front

BURN WORLD-WIDE LTD. (USA)

BURN WORLD-WIDE LTD. (USA)
CD, AD, D: David L. Clarke DF: Burn World-Wide Ltd. *Graphic Design Firm*

11718 Barrington Ct. Suite 122
Los Angeles, California 90049

PH 310.203.4993 FX 310.476.6406
E-MAIL robert@greenhood.com

Robert C. Greenhood

NEW MEDIA & TECHNOLOGY

GREENHOOD AND COMPANY (USA)
CD, AD: Petrula Vrontikis D: Samuel Lising DF: Vrontikis Design Office
Computer Equipment Consultants

MLINAR DESIGN BNO (Netherlands)
AD, D: Edvard Mlinar DF: Mlinar Design *Design Firm*

the OGGO store

WENDY
ARNETT

BANKER'S HALL
THIRD FLOOR
332, 315 - 8TH AV SW
CALGARY AB T2P 4K1

TEL   403 264 6446
FAX   403 262 9142

THE OGGO STORE (Canada)
AD: Ronald Bills D: Tina Houston, Stewart Publishing DF: McIntyre Bills Corporation
Home & Office Accessories Retailer

INSTITUTE OF DYES a. ORGANIC PRODUCTS
29 A. Struga street 95-100 ZGIERZ, POLAND

C? DIGITAL STUDIO (Indonesia)
AD, D: Andi Surja Boediman DF: C? Digital Studio
Graphic Design Firm

INSTITUTE OF DYES a. ORGANIC PRODUCTS
29 A. Struga street 95-100 ZGIERZ, POLAND

IBPO (Poland)
CD, AD, D, CW: Tadeusz Piechura DF: Atelier Tadeusz Piechura
Institute of Dyes & Organic Products

有限会社フロッグマン 〒107 東京都港区北青山2-10-18 G-フラット北青山202号
TEL.03(5411)6105 FAX.03(5411)6106

FROGMAN (Japan)
AD, D: Akihiko Ishizuki *Advertising Production*

C? DIGITAL STUDIO (Indonesia)

NOAH (Germany)
CD, AD, D, CW: Silke Löhmann / René Wynands DF: Oktober-Kommunikationsdesign
Multimedia Agency

MEDIO INC. (Japan)
CD, AD, D: Kazunobu Kitakoga DF: Medio Inc.
Design & Radio Pragram Production

HF COM. LTD. (Japan)
CD: Hidetoshi Mitsusada AD, D, I: Hironobu Mitsusada DF: UNIT
Motorsports Promoter

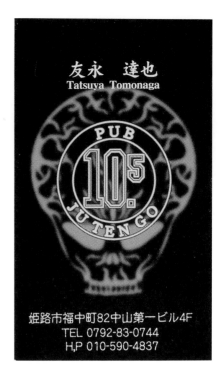

10.5 (Japan)
CD, AD, D: Hiroko Edo DF: Design Office OO1
Pub

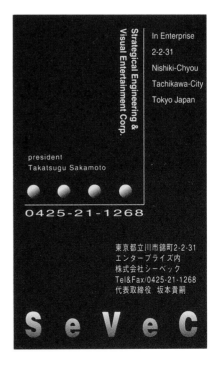

SEVEC (Japan)
D: Takatsugu Sakamoto *Visual
Entertainment Company*

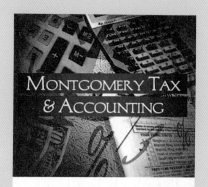

SUK J. LEE, CPA, MBA
M A N A G E R

4500 AVAMERE STREET

BETHESDA, MD 20814

PHONE: 301•897•9694

FAX: 301•897•4939

MONTGOMERY TAX & ACCOUNTING (USA)
CD, AD, D, I: Michael J. James DF: The Designpond
Accountant

Kornel Knöpfle
Diplom-Physiker

Lauteschlägerstraße 11
64289 Darmstadt
Telefon privat   06151- 711074
Telefon geschäftlich   06151- 163680

KORNEL KNÖPFLE (Germany)
D: Kerstin Antony DF: K. Antony Kommunikationsdesign *Physician*

Kornel Knöpfle ___   Lauteschlägerstraße ¹¹
                 =   64289 Darmstadt
Diplom-Physiker   Telefon ᵖʳⁱᵛᵃᵗ   06151-711074
                       Telefon ᵍᵉˢᶜʰᵃᶠᵗˡⁱᶜʰ 06151-163680

KORNEL KNÖPFLE (Germany)
D: Kerstin Antony DF: K. Antony Kommunikationsdesign *Physician*

» Unser schönster Schmuck sind die Zähne «
(Deutsches Sprichwort)

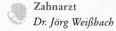 Zahnarzt
      Dr. Jörg Weißbach

Bornwiesenweg 40
61184 Karben/Rendel
fon *06039*.45190
fax *06174*.931344

DR. JÖRG WEISSBACH (Germany)
AD, D: Kerstin Antony
DF: K. Antony Kommunikationsdesign *Personal*

Kornel Knöpfle   Diplom-Physiker

      ⎡ Lauteschlägerstraße 11
      ⎢ 64289 Darmstadt
  =   ⎢ Telefon ᵖʳⁱᵛᵃᵗ   06151- 711074   ⎤
      ⎣ Telefon ᵍᵉˢᶜʰᵃᶠᵗˡⁱᶜʰ 06151- 163680 ⎦

KORNEL KNÖPFLE (Germany)
D: Kerstin Antony DF: K. Antony Kommunikationsdesign *Physician*

MATTHIAS SCHÄFER DESIGN (Germany)
CD, AD: Matthias Schäfer DF: Matthias Schäfer Design *Design Firm*

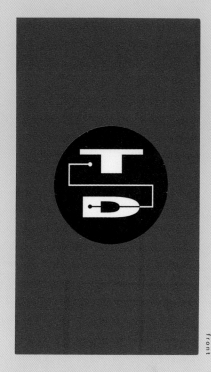

front

TIM DOTY PHOTOGRAPHY (USA)
CD, D: Greg Walters DF: Greg Walters Design
Photographer

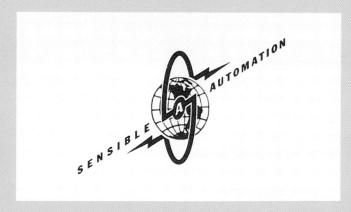

SENSIBLE AUTOMATION (USA)
CD: Kevin Wade D: Martha Graettinger DF: Planet Design Company
Consultants

YUMI SAITO (Japan)
AD, D: Takeshi Nishimura DF: Completo Inc.
Hair & Make-up Artist

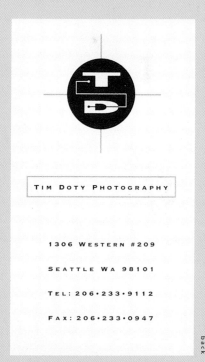

back

TIM DOTY PHOTOGRAPHY (USA)

front

back

VAN SLOUN RAMAEKERS (Netherlands)
CD, AD, D: Rob Stahl D: Annebeth Nies DF: Stahl Design *Eye Photographer*

VAN SLOUN RAMAEKERS (Netherlands)

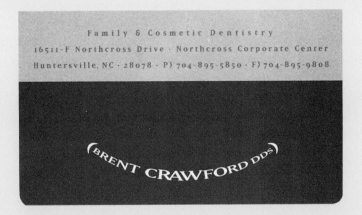

CASE STUDY SHOP #1 (Japan)
D: Massimo Vignelli *Interior Shop*

BRENT CRAWFORD DDS (USA)
AD, D: Brett Stiles DF: GSD + M *Dentist*

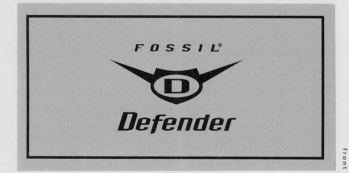

front

back

FOSSIL (USA)
CD: Tim Hale D: Andrea Levitan DF: Fossil Design
Accessories & Fashion Designer

FOSSIL (USA)

back

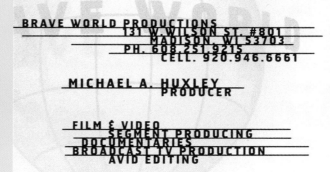

front

BRAVE WORLD PRODUCTIONS (USA)

BRAVE WORLD PRODUCTIONS (USA)
CD: Kevin Wade D: Dan Ibarra DF: Planet Design Company
Film Production

4497 South 134th Place
Tukwila, Washington 98168
Tel: (206) 242-1687
Fax: (206) 242-1897

Tony Jo Smith

24 Holyrood Drive Vermont
Victoria 3133 Australia
Phone: 03 9874 5355
Facsimile: 03 9874 7288
Mobile: 015 825 752
Email: walkerg@netspace.com.au

WAGTAIL (USA)
CD, D: Greg Walters DF: Greg Walters Design *Exhibit Design Firm*

PRICE WALKER CONSULTING (Australia)
CD, AD, D: Phil Ellett I: Andy Hook DF: Cozzolino Ellett Design D'Vision
Financial Management Company

back

front

CABO VERDE (Japan)
AD, D: Sachi Sawada DF: "Moss" Design Unit *Fashion Retailer*

CABO VERDE (Japan)

SUITE
OPTIONS

CORPORATE APARTMENTS

Debbie Holt
RELOCATION SPECIALIST

front

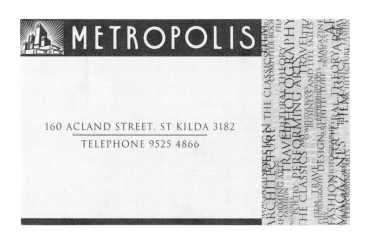

8191 Birchwood Ct., Ste. A • Johnston, IA 50131

Tel 515-252-8950 • *Fax* 515-276-5454

1-800-497-3144 • www.suiteoptions.com

back

SUITE OPTIONS (USA)
CD, AD: Sonia Greteman AD, D: Craig Tomson DF: Greteman Group
Corporate Apartments Company

SUITE OPTIONS (USA)

Berbee Information Networks Corporation
5520 Research Park Drive
Madison, Wisconsin 53711–5377
608.288.3000, extension 1202
608.288.3007, fax

BERBEE

Scott Fields
Editor
fields@berbee.com

BERBEE INFORMATION NETWORKS (USA)
CD: Kevin Wade D: Jamie Karlin DF: Planet Design Company
Internet Services Provider

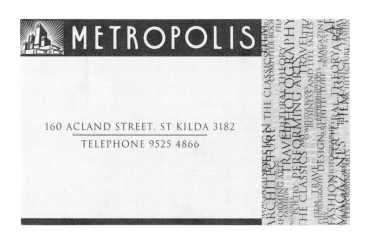

METROPOLIS

160 ACLAND STREET, ST KILDA 3182
TELEPHONE 9525 4866

METROPOLIS (Australia)
CD, AD, D: Andrew Hoyne DF: Hoyne Design *Bookshop*

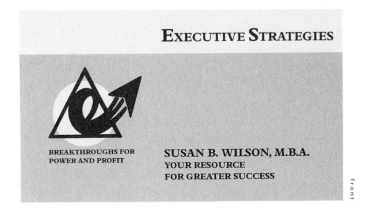

EXECUTIVE STRATEGIES

BREAKTHROUGHS FOR
POWER AND PROFIT

SUSAN B. WILSON, M.B.A.
YOUR RESOURCE
FOR GREATER SUCCESS

front

EXECUTIVE STRATEGIES (USA)
CD, AD, D, I: John Sayles DF: Sayles Graphic Design
Business Consultant

1105 W. 12TH STREET SOUTH
NEWTON, IOWA 50208

515 791 7904
888 246 GOAL
FAX 515 792 1956
ONLINE
suwilson@netins.net

back

EXECUTIVE STRATEGIES (USA)

1. NEXTRX CORPORATION (USA) AD, D: John Hornall D: Mary Hermes / Mary Chin Hutchison / David Bates DF: Hornall Anderson Design Works, Inc.
Medical System Manufacturer
2. TRANSPOINT CORPORATION (USA) AD: John Hornall D: Katha Dalton / Holly Finlayson DF: Hornall Anderson Design Works, Inc.
Computer System Provider
3. DOOKIM INC. (Korea) CD, CW: Doo Kim DF: DOOKIM Inc. *Design Firm*

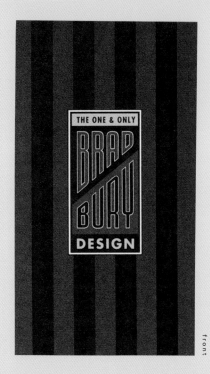

INTERACTIVE DIMENSIONS (Australia)
CD, AD, D: Rick Lambert DF: Rick Lambert Design
Exhibit Design & Construction Company

VIALOGIK (USA)
CD, AD: Sonia Greteman AD, D: Craig Tomson
Production Artist: Jo Quillin DF: Greteman Group
Technical Staff Service Company

BRADBURY DESIGN INC. (Canada)
CD, AD, D: Catharine Bradbury DF: Bradbury
Design Inc. *Graphic Design Firm*

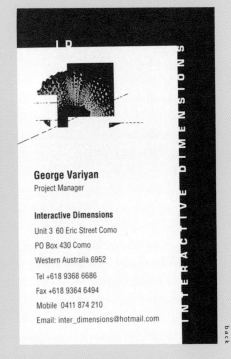

INTERACTIVE DIMENSIONS (Australia)

VIALOGIK (USA)

BRADBURY DESIGN INC. (Canada)

THE TOKYO RESTAURANT (Japan) CD: Masahisa Sakamoto D: Mayumi Murokawa DF: Hermes Inc. *Restaurant*

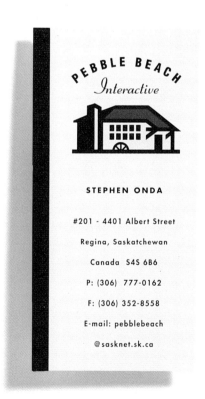

PEBBLE BEACH INTERACTIVE (Canada)
CD, AD, D: Catharine Bradbury DF: Bradbury
Design Inc. *Educational Multimedia
Company*

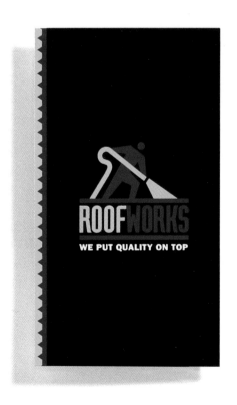

ROOF WORKS (USA)
CD, AD, D: Sonia Greteman D: James Strange DF:
Greteman Group *Roof Repairing Firm*

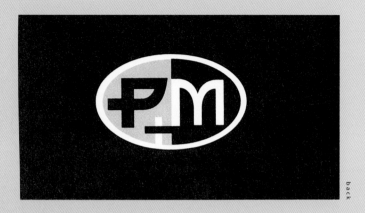

back

PETERS & MAURER (Netherlands)

front

PETERS & MAURER (Netherlands)
D: Pieter Woudt DF: Big Bolt Graphics *Industrial Design Firm*

BARRETT RUDICH (USA)
CD, AD, D, I: Jeff Fisher DF: Jeff Fisher LogoMotives *Photographer*

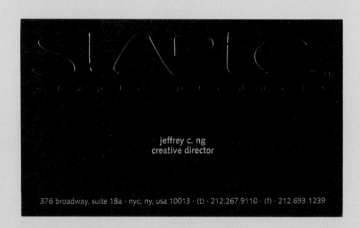

STAPLE PRODUCTS (USA)
CD, CW: Jeffrey C. Ng AD: Yuka Iwakoshi DF: Staple Products
Fashion Design Company

PMK LOGISTICS (Canada)
CD, AD, D: Catharine Bradbury DF: Bradbury Design Inc.
Trucking Company

ESTUDIO INFINITO (Brazil)
CD, AD, D: Ruth Klotzel DF: Estudio Infinito *Design Firm*

STIFTUNG UMWELT-EINSATZ SCHWEIZ (Switzerland)
CD, AD, D: Lucia Frey / Heinz Wild DF: Wild & Frey
Environmental Protection Foundation

HELEN HAWKES (Australia)
CD, AD: Andrew Hoyne P: Tash Schroter DF: Hoyne Design
Journalist

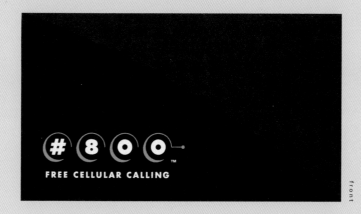

TOLL-FREE CELLULAR (USA)
AD, D: John Hornall D: Heidi Favour / Jana Nishi / Julie Lock / Mary Chin Hutchison /
Bruce Branson-Meyer DF: Hornall Anderson Design Works, Inc.
Supplier of Non-Charging Cellular Phone Numbers

TOLL-FREE CELLULAR (USA)

NEVER TOO MUCH PRODUCTIONS (Japan)
CD, AD, D: Tabito Mizuo *Music Production*

THE ARTISTS' MUSEUM (Poland)
CD, AD, D: Tadeusz Piechura CW: Ryszard Wasko DF: Atelier Tadeusz Piechura *Museum*

1

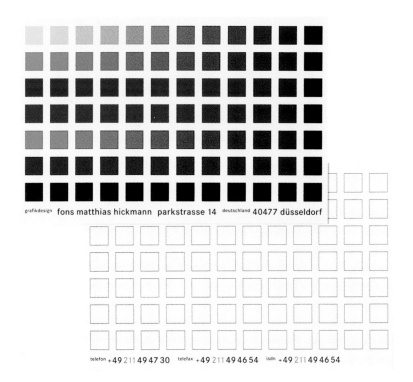

FONS M. HICKMANN (Germany)
AD, D: Fons M. Hickmann DF: Fons M. Hickmann Design *Designer*

2

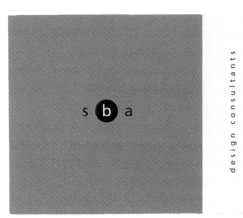

3

SOPHIE BARTHO & ASSOCIATES (Australia)
AD, D: Sophie Bartho DF: Sophie Bartho & Associates
Design Consultants

RADIX MARKETING (Canada)
CD, AD, D: Catharine Bradbury DF: Bradbury Design Inc.
Marketing Company

Macintosh Output Service Bureau

Printing

and

Design

PROP

front

Macintosh
Output Service Bureau
Printing
and
Design

PROP GRAPHIC STATION INC.

YOSHIKAZU NAMBU
President

back

PROP GRAPHIC STATION INC. (Japan)
AD: Yoshikazu Nambu D: Kayoko Sano
Design & Printing Service Company

PROP GRAPHIC STATION INC. (Japan)

Shoko Kuzuhata
Phone/Fax 0425-94-XXXX
XXXMinamidaira 1-chome,
Hino-si, Tokyo 191, Japan.
葛畑祥子 Writer
東京都日野市南平XXXXX ✉191

松本祐亮 Photographer
Masaaki Matsumoto
#201. XXXX KAMI-YOGA
6-CHOME, SETAGAYA-KU
TOKYO 158-0098, JAPAN
東京都世田谷区上用賀6-XXXX-201
TELEPHONE/03-3428-XXXX

SHOKO KUZUHATA (Japan)
AD, D: Shigeru Kanematsu DF: O-Five Remix *Writer*

MASAAKI MATSUMOTO (Japan)
AD, D: Shigeru Kanematsu DF: O-Five Remix *Photographer*

HARUO MATSUYA
2-21-1-704 Tomigaya Shibuya-ku
Tokyo 151-0063 Japan
Phone&Fax: 81-3-5454-4744
PHOTOGRAPHER

back

松谷椿土
〒151·0063
東京都渋谷区富ケ谷2·21·1
駒場マンション704
Phone&Fax:03·5454·4744
Mbl:090·1404·8325

front

HARUO MATSUYA (Japan)

HARUO MATSUYA (Japan)
AD, D: Gen Hosoya DF: Vision Inc. *Photographer*

WBP-LANDSCHAFTSARCHITEKTUR (Germany)
CD, AD, D, CW: Silke Löhmann / René Wynands DF: Oktober Kommunikationsdesign
Landscape Architect

Elisabeth Pawelec
Dipl.-Volkswirtin

Rosenbergstraße 50/1 · 70176 Stuttgart
Tel 0711.6 36 44 81 · Fax 0711.6 36 48 30

E. PAWELEC (Germany)
CD, AD, D, I, CW: Oliver A. Krimmel / Anja Oslerwalder DF: i-d Buero
Tax-Consultant

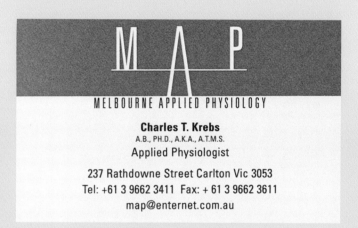

MELBOURNE APPLIED PHYSIOLOGY (Australia)
CD: Mimmo Cozzolino AD, D: Darren Ledwich DF: Cozzolino Ellett Design D'Vision
Applied Physiologist

ABERNETHY OWENS (Australia)
CD, D: David Taylor AD: Rick Lambert P: Leon Bird
DF: Rick Lambert Design *Optometrists*

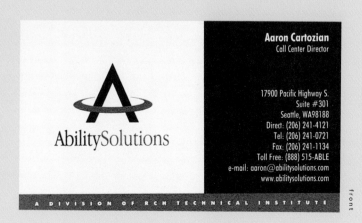

ABILITY SOLUTIONS (USA)
CD, D: Greg Walters DF: Greg Walters Design *Business Call Center*

ABILITY SOLUTIONS (USA)

COLBAR QSR (Australia)
CD: Mimmo Cozzolino AD, D, I: Darren Ledwich DF: Cozzolino Ellett Design D'Vision
Personal Products Contract Manufacturers

TIPS IRON & STEEL COMPANY (USA)
CD, AD, D, I: Mark Brinkman DF: Sibley/Peteet Design
Iron & Steel Fabrication Company

ED DYE (USA)
AD, D: John Latin DF: Skidmore Inc.
Illustrator

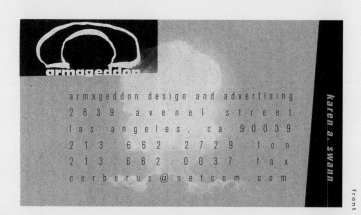

ARMAGEDDON DESIGN AND ADVERTISING (USA)
DF: Armageddon Design & Advertising *Design & Advertising Firm*

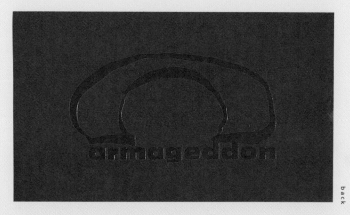

ARMAGEDDON DESIGN AND ADVERTISING (USA)

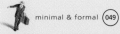

TODD SANDERS (USA) D: Todd Sanders DF: Foundation *System Consultant, Publisher & Website Designer*

PEACE COUNCIL (USA)
CD: Daniel Russ AD, D: Brett Stiles DF: GSD + M *Non-Profit Organization*

C RUSSELL & COMPANY (USA)
CD, AD: Sonia Greteman AD, D: James Strange DF: Greteman Group
Public Relations Consultancy

CODESIC (USA)
CD, AD, D, I: Lonnie Weis DF: Weis Design
Telecommunications Company

CODESIC (USA)

I-D BUERO (Germany)
CD, AD, D, I, CW: Oliver A. Krimmel / Anja Oslerwalder DF: i-d Buero
Graphic Design Firm

I-D BUERO (Germany)

PLANET CREATION OFFICE (Hong Kong)
CD, AD, D, I: Andy Lau Sing Yau DF: Planet Creation Office
Advertising & Design Firm

PLANET CREATION OFFICE (Hong Kong)

BRADLEY D. WOODS
WOODS@FUSETEC.COM

FUSE TECHNOLOGIES, INC.
4405 CHEROKEE DRIVE
MADISON, WISCONSIN 53711
TEL: 608.877.9311
FAX: 608.877.9312

front

FUSE TECHNOLOGIES (USA)
CD: Kevin Wade D: Martha Graettinger
DF: Planet Design Company
Internet Services Provider

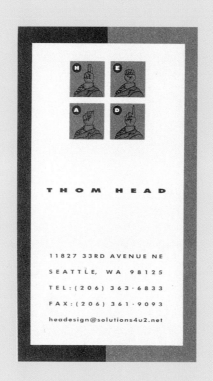

THOM HEAD

11827 33RD AVENUE NE
SEATTLE, WA 98125
TEL:(206) 363-6833
FAX:(206) 361-9093
headesign@solutions4u2.net

THOM HEAD DESIGN (USA)
CD, D: Greg Walters DF: Greg Walters Design
Exhibit Designer

Michael Watkins
President

CONCErTa

Concerta Consulting Inc.
5628 Fleming Street
Vancouver, BC V5P 3G2

t 604.324.5900
f 604.324.5901

mwatkins@concerta.com
www.concerta.com

front

CONCERTA CONSULTING INC. (Canada)
AD: Troy Bailly / Stephen Parkes D: Devid Papineau
DF: Prototype Design *Software Management Company*

back

FUSE TECHNOLOGIES (USA)

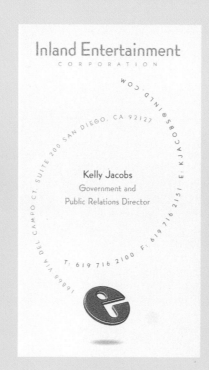

Inland Entertainment
CORPORATION

Kelly Jacobs
Government and
Public Relations Director

18668 VIA DEL CAMPO CT. SUITE 200 SAN DIEGO, CA 92127
T: 619 716 2100 F: 619 716 2151 E: KJACOBS@INLD.COM
WWW.INLD.COM

INLAND ENTERTAINMENT (USA)
CD, AD, D: José A. Serrano D, I: Miguel Perez
DF: Mires Design, Inc. *Entertainment Company*

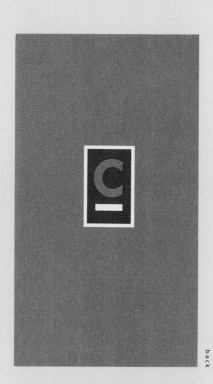

back

CONCERTA CONSULTING INC. (Canada)

SIXTY FIVE (Japan)
CD, AD, D: Tabito Mizuo *Casting Office*

VESPUCCI (Japan)
CD, AD, D: Tabito Mizuo *Fashion Retailer*

POLY WATCH GROUP LIMITED (Hong Kong)
AD: Gabriel Tsang D: Iris Kwok DF: Tupos Design Company
Watch Retail Chain Store

CICADA PROMOTION (Austria)
CD: Thomas Koch DF: The Lounge
Music Promoter

GRECA-ARTES GRÁFICAS (Portugal)
AD, D: Emanuel Barbosa DF: Vestigio
Printing House

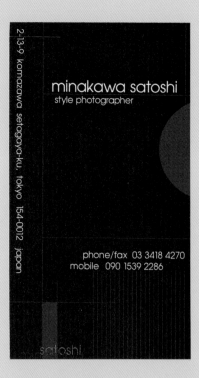

SATOSHI MINAKAWA (Japan)
D: Yukiya Shimba *Photographer*

RAPID PLAN (Germany)
CD, AD, D: Oliver A. Krimmel / Anja Oslerwalder DF: i-d Buero
CAD Software Company

RAPID PLAN (Germany)

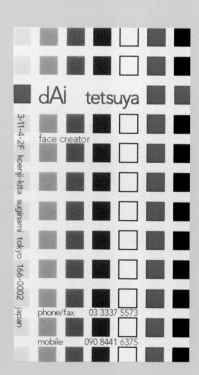

TETSUYA DAI (Japan)
D: Yukiya Shimba
Typeface Designer

KSM ZURZACH (Switzerland)
CD, AD: Lucia Frey / Heinz Wild DF: Wild & Frey
Clinic for Sleeping Disorders

MID-CONTINENT INSTRUMENTS (USA)
CD, AD: Sonia Greteman AD, D: James Strange DF: Greteman Group
Flight Instruments Maker

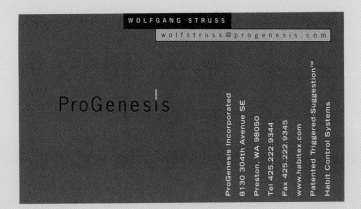

BAUHAUS INC. (Japan)
AD, D: Katsunori Watanabe DF: bauhaus Inc. *Design Firm*

ProGenesis

PROGENESIS (USA)
D: Dale Hart DF: Widmeyer Design *Medical Technology Company*

ENERSHOP (USA)
CD, AD: Rex Peteet AD, D, I: Mark Brinkman
DF: Sibley/Peteet Design *Utility Management Consultants*

ROR (USA)
CD, D: Mamoru Shimokochi D: Anne Reeves DF:
Shimokochi/Reeves *Production Studio*

RYOKO YOSHIKAWA (Japan)
AD, D: Isamu Nakazawa DF: drop *Architect*

AMG (Germany)
D: Reinhard Raich
Medical Service Company

MENK COMPUTERGAMES (Germany)
CD, AD: Matthias Schäfer DF: Matthias Schäfer Design
Computer Game Company

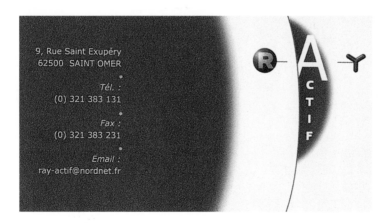

RAY-ACTIF (France)
CD, D: Jean-Jacques Tachdjian DF: i comme image *Light Company*

RAY-ACTIF (France)

NET FACILITIES GROUP (Netherlands)
CD, AD, D: R. Verkaart DF: Stoere Binken Design
Internet Publishers

KAZTECHNOLOGIES (USA)
CD: Kevin Wade D: Jamie Karlin DF: Planet
Design Company *Suspension Engineers*

Z CLUB (USA)
D: Sandy Gin DF: Sandy Gin Design
Nightclub

STOERE BINKEN DESIGN (Netherlands)
CD, AD, D: J. Borrenbergs DF: Stoere Binken Design
Graphic Design Studio

VARIETY MEDIA (UK) CD, AD: Andy Ewan D: Stephanie Fletcher P: James Mealing DF: Design Narrative *Publisher*

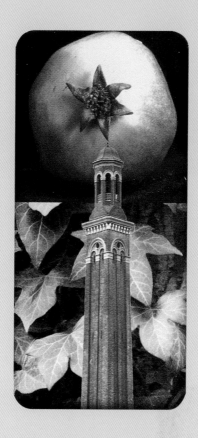

MILLER GANG INC. (USA)
CD, D, I: Mark Murphy DF: Murphy Design *Music Production Company*

MILLER GANG INC. (USA)

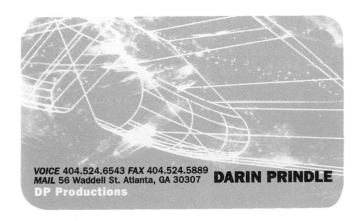

DP PRODUCTIONS (USA)
CD, AD: Derek Lerner CD, AD, D, I: Peter Rentz CD, AD, I: Sadek Bazaraa
DF: Graphic Havoc AVA *Music Production Studio*

DIERENKLINIEK KUSTERS (Netherlands)
CD, AD, D: J. Borrenbergs DF: Stoere Binken Design *Veterinary Clinic*

DON JOHNSTON (USA)
CD, AD, D: John Latin P: Don Johnston I: Dan Christie, Eyeball Graphic
DF: Skidmore Inc. *Photographer*

DON JOHNSTON (USA)

BIG BOLT GRAPHICS (USA)
D, I: Pieter Woudt DF: Big Bolt Graphics *Design Firm*

BIG BOLT GRAPHICS (USA)

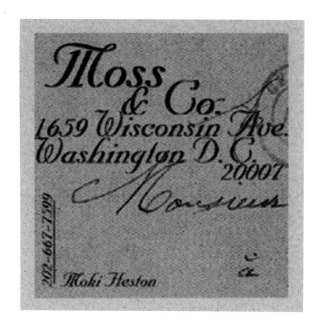

MOSS AND CO. (USA)
CD, AD, D: Moki Heston DF: Aeon Designs *Retail Shop*

9353 (USA)
CD, AD, D, I: Moki Heston DF: Aeon Designs *Bar*

SHARON GLASSMAN (USA)
D: Pieter Woudt CW: Sharon Glassman DF: Big Bolt Graphics *Copywriter*

bless, next life, future world

4E-5 2-10-21 Mita Meguro-ku Tokyo 153-0062 Japan
Tel & Fax : 03.3719.7851 / E-mail : anoyo@mosaic.com
http://www.mosaic.com/anoyo

bless, next life, future world

4E-5 2-10-21 Mita Meguro-ku Tokyo 153-0062 Japan
Tel & Fax : 03.3719.7851 / E-mail : anoyo@mosaic.com
http://www.mosaic.com/anoyo

bless, next life, future world

4E-5 2-10-21 Mita Meguro-ku Tokyo 153-0062 Japan
Tel & Fax : 03.3719.7851 / E-mail : anoyo@mosaic.com
http://www.mosaic.com/anoyo

bless, next life, future world

4E-5 2-10-21 Mita Meguro-ku Tokyo 153-0062 Japan
Tel & Fax : 03.3719.7851 / E-mail : anoyo@mosaic.com
http://www.mosaic.com/anoyo

ANOYO (Japan) AD, D: Yoshitaka Sato *Creative Team*

1. CISNEROS TELEVISION GROUP (USA) CD, D: Carolina Bilbao D: Vanessa Eckstein *Television Production*
2. Ll12 (Belgium) CD, AD, D: Frederic Vanhorenbeke DF: Coast *Restaurant*

SEBASTIAAN BAMS ASSURANTIËN (Netherlands)
CD, AD, D: J. Borrenbergs DF: Stoere Binken Design *Insurance Company*

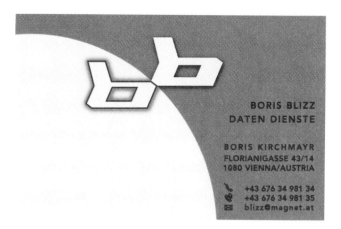

BORIS KIRCHMAYR (Austria)
CD: Thomas Koch DF: The Lounge *Computer Support Company*

YOGATOPIA (USA)
CD, AD: Petrula Vrontikis D: Susan Carter DF: Vrontikis Design Office
Yoga Studio

YOGATOPIA (USA)

IGNITION (USA)

IGNITION (USA)
CD: John Swieter CD, D: Mark Ford DF: Swieter Design U. S.
Industrial Design Firm

GYRATE INTERNET SOLUTIONS (USA)

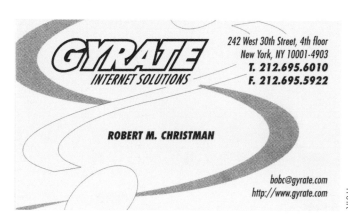

GYRATE INTERNET SOLUTIONS (USA)
D: Tim Morse DF: Coloured Hard Inc.
Website Development Company

HERO BRANDS LTD. (USA)
CD, D: Mark Murphy DF: Murphy Design
Licensing & Branding Company

HERO BRANDS LTD. (USA)

D4 CREATIVE GROUP (USA)

D4 CREATIVE GROUP (USA)
AD, D: Wicky W. Lee DF: D4 Creative Group *Advertising Agency*

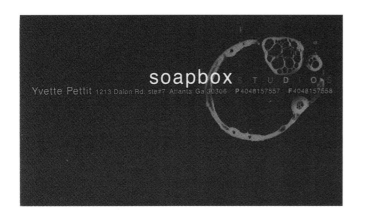

SOAP BOX STUDIOS (USA)
CD, AD, D, I: Derek Lerner DF: Graphic Havoc AVA
Audio Post Production

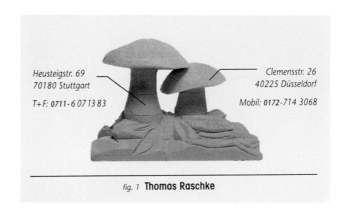

fig. 1 **Thomas Raschke**

THOMAS RASCHKE (Germany)
CD, AD, D, P, I, CW: Oliver A. Krimmel / Anja Oslerwalder DF: i-d Buero
Sculptor

SNOECK (Netherlands)
CD, D, P: Arno Bauman DF: Studio Bauman BNO
Electric Appliances *Wholesaler*

BLUECON (Austria)
CD: Thomas Koch DF: The Lounge *Trading Company*

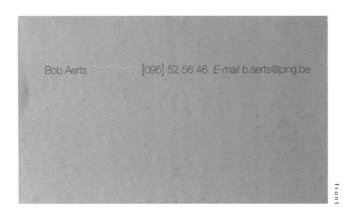

front

BOB AERTS (Belgium)
CD, AD, D: Frederic Vanhorenbeke DF: Coast *Architect*

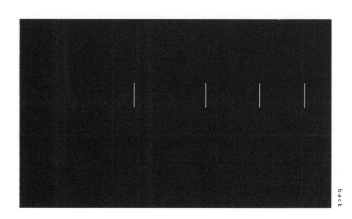

back

BOB AERTS (Belgium)

SUPER NATURAL DESIGN (USA) CD, AD, D: Hajdeja Ehline CD, AD: Christie Riyford DF: Super-Natural Design *Design Firm*

MICHIKO KAKUTA (Japan)
D: Kazunori Sadahiro I: Michiko Kakuta *Illustrator*

BEAR MUSIC FACTORY (Germany)
CD, AD, D, P, I, CW: Oliver A. Krimmel / Anja Oslerwalder DF: i-d Buero
Music Management Company

MENTALWORKS STUDIO (Singapore)
DF: Mentalworks Studio *Animation, Multimedia & Design Studio*

IBIZA MEDITERRANEAN (Australia)
AD: Glenn Gould D: Dani Abel DF: Kajun Design Pty Ltd. *Restaurant*

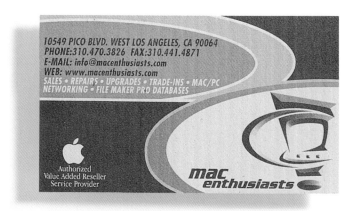

MAC ENTHUSIASTS (USA)
AD, D: Patty Palazzo DF: T. T. P. Art *Computer Retailer*

DROP TYPOGRAFIX (Japan)
CD, AD, D: Isamu Nakazawa DF: drop
Typographics & Design Firm

YOSH NASH DESIGN (Netherlands)
CD, AD, D: R. Verkaart DF: Stoere Binken Design *Design Firm*

SWIETER DESIGN U.S. (USA)
CD: John Swieter CD, D: Mark Ford DF: Swieter Design U. S.
Multi-Disciplinary Communications Firm

SWIETER DESIGN U.S. (USA)

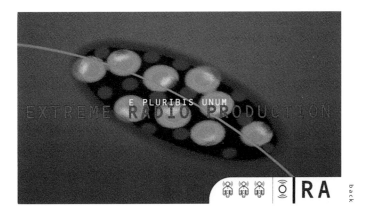

RADIO ACTIVE (USA)

RADIO ACTIVE (USA)
CD, AD, D, I: Carlos Segura DF: Segura Inc.
Radio Production Company

KESSELSKRAMER (Netherlands) CD, AD: Erik Kessels CD, CW: Johan Kramer DF: Kesselskramer *Advertising Agency*

[THREE] (USA)
CD, AD, D, P: Robert Paul Nixon DF: [three]
Design Firm

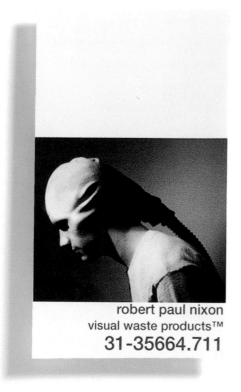

[THREE] (USA)
CD, AD, D, P, I: Robert Paul Nixon DF: [three]
Design Firm

[THREE] (USA)
CD, AD, D, P: Robert Paul Nixon DF: [three]
Design Firm

[THREE] (USA)
CD, AD, D, P: Robert Paul Nixon DF: [three]
Design Firm

LE LABOMATIC (France) CD, AD, D, P, CW: Sylvie Astié DF: Le Labomatic *Graphic Design Firm*

1. CHRISTIAN ASCHMAN (Belgium) DF: Signé Lazer *Photographer*
2. PETER NENCINI (Belgium) AD, D, P: Peter Nencini *Designer*

ARTVILLE (USA) CD: Kevin Wade D: Martha Graettinger DF: Planet Design Company *Stock Images Agency*

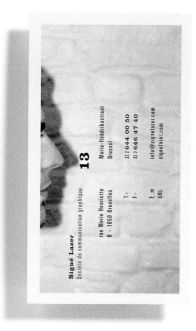
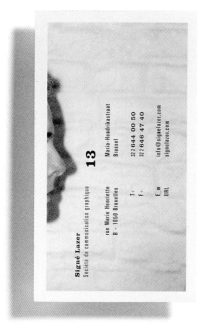
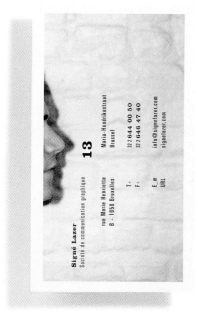
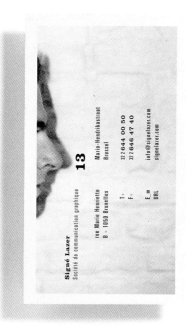
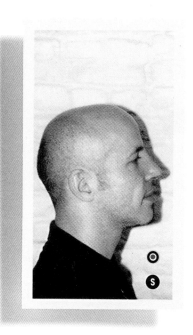

SIGNÉ LAZER (Belgium) DF: Signé Lazer Graphic *Design Firm*

container rec.
reeperbahn 115
20359 hamburg

hardy storz
spiritus rector

fon 040 - 317 960 60
fax 040 - 317 42 22

container rec.
reeperbahn 115
20359 hamburg

acidambientdrum'n'basselectro goahardcore
hiphophouse progressivetrance&triphop
vinyl&compactdiscs plattenkoffertaschenzubehör
kartenvorverkauf, mangas, t'shirts &
schicken schnickschnack,

mo. - sa. 13 - 21⁰⁰ uhr
so. 15 - 21 uhr
fon 040 - 317 44 22
fax 040 - 317 42 22

the passion of being today

CONTAINER (Gemany) DF: Dice Record Company

DICE (Germany) DF: Dice *Design Firm*

DOLL WERBETEAM (Germany) DF: Dice *Advertising Agency*

ARNOLD & BIERBRAUER (Germany)
CD, AD, D, P, I, CW: Oliver A. Krimmel / Anja Oslerwalder DF: i-d Buero
Design Firm

COLOURED HARD INC. (USA)
CD, D: Tim Morse DF: Coloured Hard Inc.
Graphic Design Firm

MG-DESIGN (Germany)
CD, AD, D, P, I, CW: Oliver A. Krimmel / Anja Oslerwalder DF: i-d Buero
Industrial Design Firm

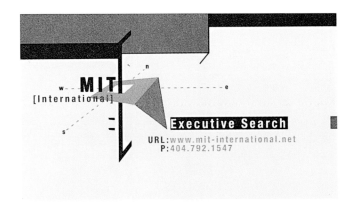

MIT INTERNATIONAL (USA)
CD, AD, D: Sadek Bazaraa DF: Graphic Havoc AVA
Staff Agency

PILGRAM (Germany)
CD, AD, D, P, I, CW: Oliver A. Krimmel / Anja Oslerwalder DF: i-d Buero
Industrial Design Firm

HI'HAT STUDIO (Japan)
CD, AD, D: Isamu Nakazawa DF: hi'hat studio
Typographics & Design Firm

NEL (Netherlands) CD: Erik Kessels / Johan Kramer AD, D: Karen Heuter P: Diverse CW: Dave Bell DF: Kesselskramer *Photographers' Agency*

JONATHAN GRIFFITHS (Netherlands) CD, AD, D: Erik Kessels CD, CW: Johan Kramer P: Kerrie Van Aarssen DF: Kesselskramer *Editor*

[THREE] (USA)
CD, AD, D, P, I: Robert Paul Nixon DF: [three]
Design Firm

[THREE] (USA)

ZONA CERO DESIGN (Mexico)
CD, AD, D, I: Teo Gonzalez P: Tuffic Yazbek DF: Zona Cero Design
Graphic Design Firm

PAUL DALY DESIGN (UK)
AD, D, P: Yuki Miyake DF: System Gafa *Furniture & Interior Design Firm*

SYSTEM GAFA (UK)
AD, D, P: Yuki Miyake DF: System Gafa
Graphic Design Firm

DIVE ARCHITECTS (UK)
AD, D: Yuki Miyake DF: System Gafa
Architect

EEVOLUTE MUZIQUE (Netherlands)
CD, AD, D: J. Borrenbergs DF: Stoere Binken Design *Techno Music Label*

FONS M. HICKMANN (Germany)
AD, D: Fons M. Hickmann DF: Fons M. Hickmann Design
Designer

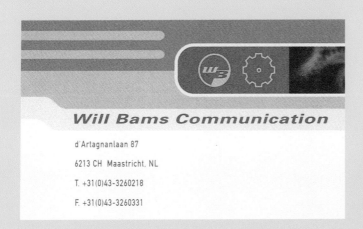

WILL BAMS COMMUNICATION (Netherlands)
CD, AD, D: J. Borrenbergs DF: Stoere Binken Design
Public Relations Company

ARGUS GMBH (Germany)
CD, AD, D, P, I, CW: Oliver A. Krimmel /
Anja Oslerwalder DF: i-d Buero
Real Estate Company

SIRIUS (Netherlands)
CD, AD, D: J. Borrenbergs / R. Verkaart
DF: Stoere Binken Design *Gallery*

SNITKER/DEHAAS (Netherlands)
AD: Michaël Snitker DF: Sniker I. C. D *Design Firm*

HORN OF PLENTY (Netherlands)
AD: Michaël Snitker DF: Sniker I. C. D *Musician*

SNITKER/BORST ARCHITECTEN (Netherlands)
AD: Michaël Snitker DF: Sniker I. C. D *Architect*

SNITKER/BORST ARCHITECTEN (Netherlands)

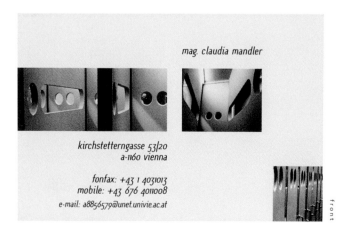

CLAUDIA MANDLER (Austria)
CD: Thomas Koch DF: The Lounge *Account Manager*

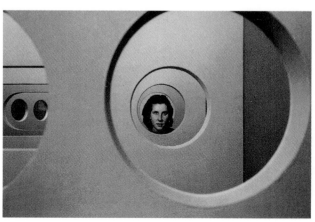

CLAUDIA MANDLER (Austria)

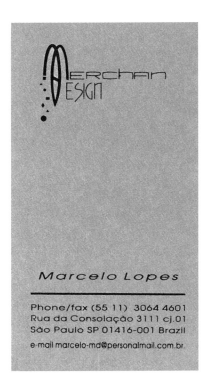

MERCHAN DESIGN (Brazil)
D: Marcelo Lopes DF: Merchan Design
Design Firm

CHROMAZONE CORPORATION LTD. (UK)
CD, D: Austin Cowdall AD: Charles Cowdall DF: NEW
Film & Advertising Company

front

DESIGN STUDIO BLUE-? (Japan)
AD, D: Koichi Shoji D: Takamasa Hatsuda
DF:design studio BLUE-? *Graphic Design Firm*

3 SOME (Netherlands)
CD, AD, D: R. Verkaart DF: Stoere Binken Design
Internet Publishers

back

DESIGN STUDIO BLUE-? (Japan)

MARTIN REINHART (Austria) CD: Thomas Koch DF: The Lounge *Video Production*

1. TAKEO ARAI OFFICE (Japan) AD, D: Gen Hosoya DF: Vision Inc. *Hair & Make-up Artist*
2. VISION INC. (Japan) AD, D: Gen Hosoya DF: Vision Inc. *Design Firm*
3. KURA KURA MUSIC (Japan) AD, D: Gen Hosoya DF: Vison Inc. *Music Production*

PLAYPEN (USA) CD, AD: Petrula Vrontikis D: Kim Sage DF: Vrontikis Design Office *Entertainment Broadcast Graphic Design Firm*

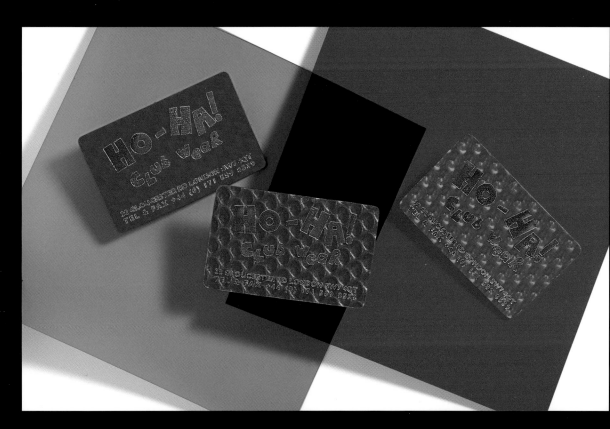

HO-HA! CLUB WEAR (UK) DF: Ho-Ha! Club Wear *Fashion Retailer*

P-L LINE (Netherlands)
CD, AD, D, I: Boy Bastiaens DF: Stormhand
Boutique

OWN SERVICES (Netherlands)
CD, AD, D, I: Boy Bastiaens DF: Stormhand
Graphic Designer

1. EMIDISC (UK) CD: Charles Cowdall AD, D: Austin Cowdall DF: NEW *Record Company*
2. LAMBIE HARPER LTD. (UK) CD, AD, D, I, CW: Austin Cowdall DF: NEW *TV Production & Advertising Firm*
3. NEW GRAPHICS/ILLUSTRATION (UK) CD, D: Austin Cowdall AD: Claive Roberts / Matt Hamilton DF: NEW
Design & Illustration Firm
4. B-MOVA (UK) CD: B-Mova / Charles Cowdall CD, AD, D, I: Matthew Hamilton DF: NEW *Musician*
5. NEW STUDIO (UK) AD, D: Austin Cowdall DF: NEW *Design & Illustration Firm*
6. B-MOVA (UK) CD, AD, D, I: Matthew Hamilton DF: NEW *Musician Management Company*

front

back

JOVEN OROZCO DESIGN (USA)
CD: Joven Orozco D: Brandon Mercado DF: Joven Orozco Design
Design Firm

front

back

JOKEN INDUSTRIES (USA)
CD, D: Joven Orozco DF: Joven Orozco Design
Greeting Card Company

ARROW PICTURES (Germany)
CD, AD, D, P, I, CW: Oliver A. Krimmel / Anja Oslerwalder
DF: i-d Buero *Film Company*

BERND KAMMERER (Germany)
CD, AD, D, P, I, CW: Oliver A. Krimmel / Anja Oslerwalder
DF: i-d Buero *Photographer*

Felix J. Gauder

elixir Gesellschaft für Medienmarketing mbH
Melittastrasse 15 • D-70597 Stuttgart
Fernruf 0711●765971 • Telekopie 0711●7655143
Unterwegs erreichbar unter 0172...741 2042

ELIXIR (Germany)
CD, AD, D, P, I, CW: Oliver A. Krimmel / Anja Oslerwalder DF: i-d Buero
Marketing Company

Arno Müller
GESCHÄFTSFÜHRER

elixir Gesellschaft für Medienmarketing mbH
Julius-Hölder-Strasse 29b • D-70597 Stuttgart
Fernruf 0711●900213 • Telekopie 0711●9002150
Elektronisches Postfach: compuserve 106212,3231

ELIXIR (Germany)
CD, AD, D, P, I, CW: Oliver A. Krimmel / Anja Oslerwalder DF: i-d Buero
Marketing Company

front

ERICA KOZOCAS

A CREATIVE COMMUNICATIONS AGENCY

400 SOUTH EL CAMINO REAL. SUITE 400.
SAN MATEO, CALIFORNIA 94402. USA.
650.548.6960 (t)   650.548.6955 (f)   EKOZOCAS@GLOWSF.COM

back

GLOW (USA)
CD, AD, D, I: Carlos Segura DF: Segura Inc. *New Media Company*

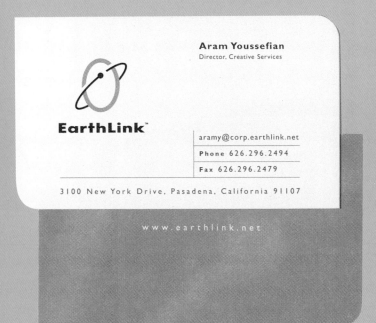

Aram Youssefian
Director, Creative Services

EarthLink™

aramy@corp.earthlink.net

Phone 626.296.2494

Fax 626.296.2479

3100 New York Drive, Pasadena, California 91107

w w w . e a r t h l i n k . n e t

EARTHLINK (USA)
CD: Aram Youssefian D: Barbara Chan DF: Earthlink, Creative Services
Internet Service Provider

GroundZero
Architecture + Fabrication

Craig A. Beneke, AIA

4901 Keller Springs Rd.   pho 972 267.0900
Suite Number 105   fax 972 267.0901
Dallas, Texas 75248   cel 972 523.1562

GroundZero

GROUND ZERO (USA)
CD, D: Mark Ford DF: Swieter Design U.S.
Architecture & Fabrication Company

1. ACTIVATE (USA) CD, AD, D: Michael Connors DF: Motive Design Research *Design Firm*
2. SHERYL SIKORA (USA) CD, AD, D, CW: Steven Sikora DF: Design Guys *Hairstylist*

40A Pagoda Street Singapore 059199 Tel/Fax: (65) 224 3851 phunkstudio@post1.com

9 258 3824
Sylvia
Tan

PHUNK STUDIO (Singapore)
D: Jackson Tan / William Chan / Alvin Tan / Melvin Chee / Perry Neo
DF: Phunk Studio *Graphic Design Firm*

ANTENNA GRAPHIC BASE (Japan)
AD, D: Akira Sumi DF: Antenna Graphic Base
Design Firm

HIROYUKI ISHIKURA (Japan)
D: Hiroyuki Ishikura *Illustrator*

SPONTANEOUS COMBUSTION (USA)
CD: Carlos Segura AD, D, I: Colin Metcalf
DF: Segura Inc. *Film Production*

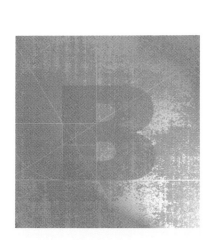

marketing

communication

design

BELYEA (USA)
CD: Patricia Belyea D: Ron Lars Hansen DF: Belyea
Marketing & Graphic Design Firm

SPONTANEOUS COMBUSTION (USA)

PICTURE TUBE (USA)
CD, AD, D, I: Randall J. Lane CD, AD, D: Derek Lerner
DF: Graphic Havoc AVA *Video Production*

WISH (USA)
CD, AD, D, I: Derek Lerner CD, AD: Randall Lane
DF: Graphic Havoc AVA *Fashion Retailer*

MACHINE (USA)
CD, AD, D: Derek Lerner DF: Graphic Havoc AVA
Artist Group

1. NASTY KAT DESIGN (USA) AD, D: Patty Palazzo DF: T.T.P. Art *Design Firm*
2. HYPERWERKS (USA) AD, D: Patty Palazzo DF: T.T.P Art *Comic Book Design Firm*
3. STUDIO 936 (USA) AD, D: Patty Palazzo DF: T.T.P. Art *Design Firm*

UPSTAIRS (Germany)
CD, AD, D, P, I, CW: Oliver A. Krimmel / Anja Oslerwalder DF: i-d Buero
Children's Wear Retailer

I-D BUERO (Germany)
CD, AD, D, P, I, CW: Oliver A. Krimmel / Anja Oslerwalder
DF: i-d Buero *Graphic Design Firm*

JORDIE R. HUDSON (USA)
CD, AD, D, P, I: David Merten DF: Graphic Havoc AVA
Artist

MATTHIAS BOHNER (Germany) CD, AD, D, P, I, CW: Oliver A. Krimmel / Anja Oslerwalder DF: i-d Buero *Industrial Designers*

FIREHOUSE PROMOTIONS (Canada)
AD: Troy Bailly / Stephen Parkes D, I: David Papineau DF: Prototype Design
Event Promotion Company

PROTOTYPE DESIGN (Canada)
AD: Troy Bailly / Stephen Parkes D, I: David Papineau DF: Prototype Design
Design Firm

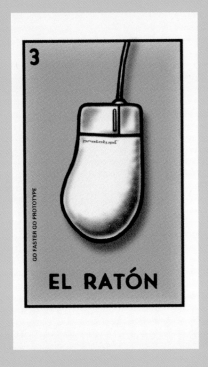

PROTOTYPE DESIGN (Canada)
AD: Troy Bailly / Stephen Parkes
D, I: David Papineau DF: Prototype Design
Design Firm

MICHAL KUBENK-CZECH (Canada)
CD: Stephen Parkes D: Troy Bailly I: David Papineau DF: Prototype Design
DJ & Musician

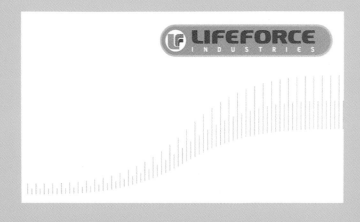

LIFEFORCE INDUSTRIES (Canada)
AD: Troy Bailly D: Stephen Parkes / David Papineau DF: Prototype Design
Event Promotor

SALISBURY STUDIOS (USA)
CD: Kevin Wade D: Raelene Mercer DF: Planet Design Company
Photographer

SALISBURY STUDIOS (USA)

SQUARE ROUTES (USA)
CD: Joven Orozco AD, D: Kenneth Lim DF: Joven Orozco Design
Greeting Card Company

REBECCA GLEASON (USA)
AD, D: John Fuller D: Andy Mueller DF: Ohio Girl
Photographer

CLICKSTREAM (Canada)
CD, AD: Catharine Bradbury D, I: Dean Bartsch DF: Bradbury Design Inc.
Website Programming Company

TYNDAL STONE MEDIA (Canada)
CD, AD: Catharine Bradbury D: Dean Bartsch DF: Bradbury Design Inc.
Educational Multimedia Company

GRAPHIC HAVOC AVISUALAGENCY (USA)
CD, AD, D: Derek Lerner CD, AD, D,
P: Sadek Bazaraa DF: Graphic Havoc AVA
Graphic Design Firm

KEITA NISHIO (Japan)
AD: Yoshitaka Sato *Photographer*

EARTH PROJECT (Japan)
AD, D, P: Takayuki Uchiyama *Beauty Salon*

ANTENNA GRAPHIC BASE (Japan)
AD, D: Akira Sumi DF: Antenna Graphic Base
Design Firm

SURGE PRODUCTIONS (Canada)
CD, AD, D: Noël Nanton D: Nick Vongthavy DF: tYPOtHERAPY + DESiGN
Event Designer & Catering Service Company

SURGE PRODUCTIONS (Canada)
CD, AD, D: Noël Nanton D: Nick Vongthavy DF: tYPOtHERAPY + DESiGN
Event Designer & Catering Service Company

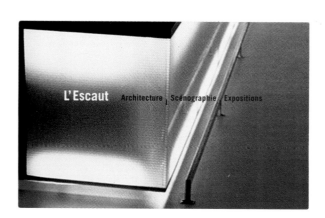

DENNIS IRWIN ILLUSTRATION (USA)
CD, AD, D, I: Dennis Irwin *Illustration Firm*

BEEF-TEC (Belgium)
AD, D: Eric Pringels *Personal*

VARIETY MEDIA (UK)
CD: Andy Ewan AD: Vibe Bangsgaard D: Alison Beake P: Peter Dazeley
DF: Design Narrative *Publisher*

BEEF-TEC (Belgium)
AD, D: Eric Pringels *Personal*

front

HAMMERQUIST & HALVERSON (USA)
AD: Jack Anderson D, I: Mike Calkins DF: Hornall Anderson Design Works, Inc.
Advertising Firm

back

HAMMERQUIST & HALVERSON (USA)

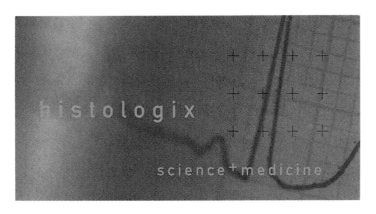

HISTOLOGIX (Netherlands)
CD, AD, D: Anne Kuban DF: Stahl Design *Phermaceutical Firm*

WHITE OUT GRAPHICS (Japan)
AD, D: Yoshitaka Sato *Graphic Design Firm*

ALVION LIMITED (Japan)
CD, AD, D, CW: Isamu Nakazawa DF: drop
Video Game Developer

RYOKO YOSHIKAWA (Japan)
AD, D: Isamu Nakazawa DF: drop *Architect*

JOVEN OROZCO DESIGN (USA) CD: Joven Orozco CW: Shirley Noda DF: Joven Orozco Design *Design Firm*

OUTDOOR NO.1 COLLECTION (Japan)
D: Outdoor No.1 Collection *Outdoor Wear Retailer*

NAOKI SAITO (Japan)
AD, D, CW: Naoki Saito *Graphic Designer*

PLANET DESIGN COMPANY (USA)
CD: Dana Lytle / Kevin Wade D: Martha Graettinger DF: Planet Design Company
Graphic Design & Advertising Firm

CSI DIGITAL (USA)
AD, D: Jack Anderson D: John Anicker DF: Hornall Anderson Design Works, Inc.
Computer Equipment Reseller

SADAHIRO KAZUNORI

front

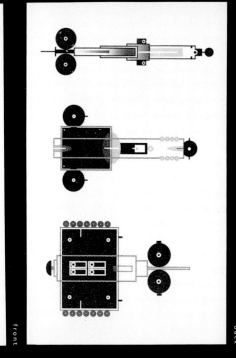

back

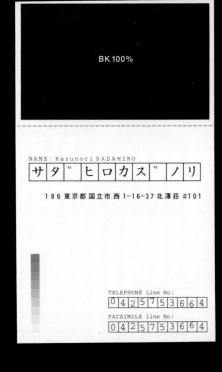

BK 100%

NAME : Kazunori SADAHIRO

サダ゛ヒロカス゛ノリ

186 東京都 国立市 西 1-16-37 北澤荘 #101

TELEPHONE Line No:
| 0 | 4 | 2 | 5 | 7 | 5 | 3 | 6 | 6 | 4 |

FACSIMILE line No:
| 0 | 4 | 2 | 5 | 7 | 5 | 3 | 6 | 6 | 4 |

front

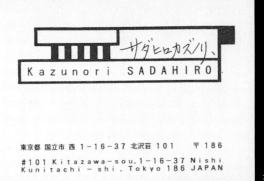

サダヒロカズノリ、
Kazunori SADAHIRO

東京都 国立市 西 1-16-37 北沢荘 101　　〒186

#101 Kitazawa-sou,1-16-37 Nishi
Kunitachi - shi , Tokyo 186 JAPAN

front

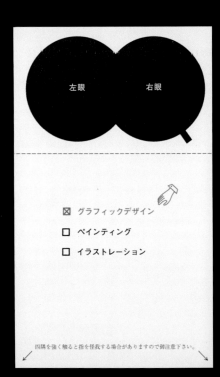

左眼　　右眼

☒ グラフィックデザイン

☐ ペインティング

☐ イラストレーション

四隅を強く触ると指を怪我する場合がありますので御注意下さい。

back

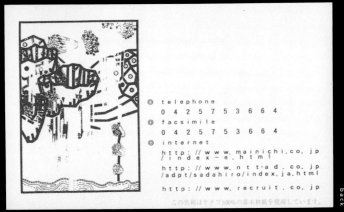

◎ telephone
0 4 2 5 7 5 3 6 6 4
◎ facsimile
0 4 2 5 7 5 3 6 6 4
◎ internet
http://www.mainichi.co.jp
/index-e.html
http://www.ntt-ad.co.jp
/adpt/sadahiro/index.ja.html
http://www.recruit.co.jp

この名刺はケナフ100%の非木材紙を使用しています。

back

市川 健治
Kenji Ichikawa

196-0003
東京都昭島市松原町5-15-10
e-mail turbine-kenji@mvj.biglobe.ne.jp

front

KENJI ICHIKAWA (Japan)

KAZUNORI SADAHIRO

JAPAN

front

KAZUNORI SADAHIRO (Japan)

KAZUNORI SADAHIRO

JAPAN

front

KAZUNORI SADAHIRO (Japan)

TELEPHONE
042・546・9761

FACSIMILE
042・546・9761

MOBILE
040・66・25238

back

KENJI ICHIKAWA (Japan)
I: Kazunori Sadahiro *Artist*

KAZUNORI SADAHIRO

JAPAN

back

KAZUNORI SADAHIRO (Japan)
D, I: Kazunori Sadahiro
Designer & Illustrator

KAZUNORI SADAHIRO

JAPAN

back

KAZUNORI SADAHIRO (Japan)
D, I: Kazunori Sadahiro
Designer & Illustrator

BERNIE SOLO (USA) AD, D: John Latin DF: Skidmore Inc. *Lamp Designer*

GOOD SPORT & EVENT GMBH (Germany)
CD, AD, D: Ruediger Goetz I: Elke Boehm
DF: Simon & Goetz Design
Sports & Event Agency

GOOD PUBLISHING & PROGRAMMING GMBH (Germany)
CD, AD, D: Ruediger Goetz I: Elke Boehm DF: Simon & Goetz Design
Publisher

GOOD SERVICE & PROMOTION GMBH (Germany)
CD, AD, D: Ruediger Goetz I: Elke Boehm DF: Simon & Goetz Design
Promotion Service Company

CO/OPERATION BETEILIGUNGS HOLDING GMBH (Germany)

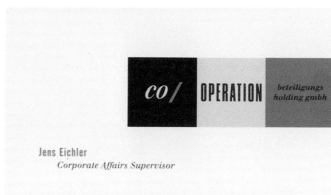

CO/OPERATION BETEILIGUNGS HOLDING GMBH (Germany)
CD, AD, D: Ruediger Goetz I: Elke Boehm DF: Simon & Goetz Design
Distribution Company

SUM SYSTEMS (USA)
CD, AD, D: Michael Connors DF: Motive Design Research
Accounting Firm

MARSHALL ALKEMADE (Australia)
CD, AD, D: Andrew Hoyne DF: Hoyne Design *Architects*

EDINGER TISCHLEREI (Austria)
CD, AD, D: Heinzle Lothar Ämilian DF: Atelier Heinzle *Carpenter*

EDINGER TISCHLEREI (Austria)

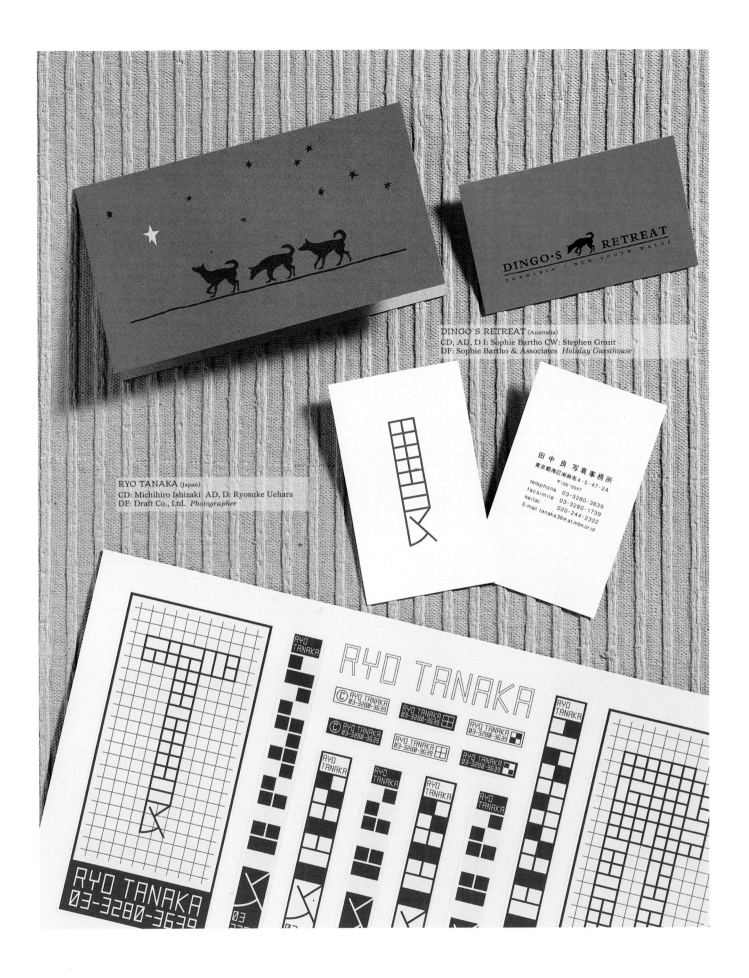

DINGO'S RETREAT (Australia)
CD, AD, D I: Sophie Bartho CW: Stephen Grant
DF: Sophie Bartho & Associates *Holiday Guesthouse*

RYO TANAKA (Japan)
CD: Michihiro Ishizaki AD, D: Ryosuke Uehara
DF: Draft Co., Ltd. *Photographer*

TRUCKWISE (Canada)

TRUCKWISE (Canada)
CD, AD: Catharine Bradbury D: Dean Bartsch DF: Bradbury Design Inc.
Software Retailer

SIERRA SUITES (USA)

SIERRA SUITES (USA)
CD, AD: Sonia Greteman AD, D: James Strange DF: Greteman Group *Hotel*

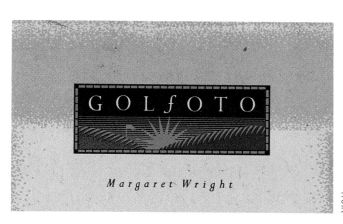

GOLFOTO (USA)

GOLFOTO (USA)
CD, AD: Sonia Greteman AD, D: James Strange Production Artist: Jo Quillin
DF: Greteman Group *Golf Photography Agency*

drs. ir. J.C. Huyghe
DIRECTEUR

2
dvlop

Willemsparkweg 221
1071 HC Amsterdam
Nederland
TEL   +31 (0)20 4711 904
FAX   +31 (0)20 4711 906
PRIVÉ +31 (0)20 4711 909
E-MAIL info@2dvlop.nl
INTERNET www.2dvlop.nl

2DVLOP VASTGOED BV

2 DVLOP (Netherlands)
CD: Arno Bauman D: Inge Van Der Ploeg
DF: Studio Bauman BNO
Real Estate Developer

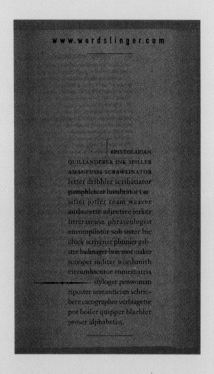

www.wordslinger.com

ΕPISTOLARIAN
QUILLANDERER INK SPILLER
AMANUSIS SCRAWLINATOR
letter dribbler scribatiator
pamphleteer humbrator ver
sifier jotler ream weaver
authorette adjective jerker
litterateuse phraseologist
encompilator sob sister bic
chick scrivener plumier gab
ster badmager bon mot maker
scooper inditer wordsmith
circumlocutor romeinatrix
styloger penwoman
riposter semantician schtie
bere cacographer verbiagette
pot boiler quipper blurbler
proser alphabetist.

BRITTANY STROMBERG (USA)
CD, AD, D, P: Denise Heckman CW: Brittany
Stromberg DF: Motive Design Research
Copywriter

BEST CELLARS™

1291 LEXINGTON AVE
NEW YORK NY 10128
TEL 212.426.4200
FAX 212.426.9597

BEST CELLARS (USA)
AD, D: Jack Anderson D: Lisa Cerveny / Jana Wilson
Esser / Nicole Bloss Logo Illustrator: David Bates
DF: Hornall Anderson Design Works, Inc.
Wine Distributor & Reseller

Mc | J
McGarrah
Jessee

Mark McGarrah

1000 Westbank Rd.
Suite 207
Austin, Texas 78746
(512) 327-5005
Fax 327-7008

MCGARRAH/JESSEE (USA)
CD, AD, D: Rex Peteet AD: Bryan Jessee
DF: Sibley/Peteet Design
Advertising Agency

W. C. WINKS HARDWARE (USA)
CD, AD, D, I: Jeff Fisher DF: Jeff Fisher LogoMotives
Hardware Retailer

THE LOUNGE (Austria)
CD: Thomas Koch DF: The Lounge *Design Firm*

THE LOUNGE (Austria)
CD: Thomas Koch DF: The Lounge *Design Firm*

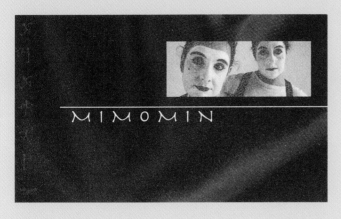

MIMOMIN (Austria)
D: Reinhard Raich *Pantomimer*

TABLEAUX LOUNGE (Japan)
CD, AD: Petrula Vrontikis D: Peggy Woo DF: Vrontikis Design Office
Restaurant

KIMI NII (Brazil)
CD, AD, D: Ruth Klotzel / Paulo Labriola DF: Estudio Infinito
Artist

THE SPEERS FILM PRODUCTION COMPANY LIMITED (Ireland)
AD, D: Peter Maybury *Film Production*

LANIE RILEY (USA)
CD, AD, D: Rick Eiber DF: Rick Eiber Design (RED)
Councelor & Massage Therapist

HOME SERVICE (Netherlands)
CD, AD, D: Rob Stahl / Annebeth Nies DF: Stahl Design
Interior Decorating Company

JAZZ IN THE PINES (USA)
CD, AD: Stan Evenson D: Mark Sojka DF: Evenson Design Group
Non-Profit Event Organizer

CANDINAS CHOCOLATIER (USA)
CD: Kevin Wade D: Martha Graettinger DF: Planet Design Company
Chocolate Maker

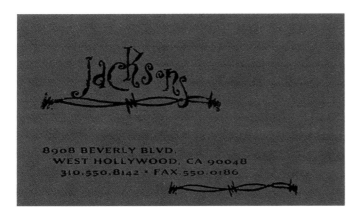

ALAN JACKSON (USA)
CD, AD: Petrula Vrontikis D: Kim Sage DF: Vrontikis Design Office
Restaurant

COR ADVISORS (USA)
CD: Kevin Wade D: Martha Graettinger
DF: Planet Design Company *Consultants*

GUILD COM (USA)
CD: Dana Lytle D: Ben Hirby
DF: Planet Design Company
Art Coordinator

CONCORD LIMOUSINE SERVICE (USA)
AD, D: Brett Stiles DF: GSD + M *Limousine Service Company*

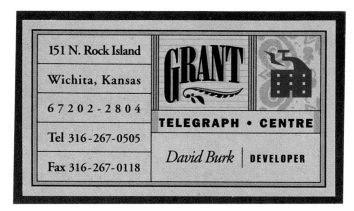

GRANT TELEGRAPH CENTRE (USA)
CD, AD: Sonia Greteman AD, D: James Strange CW: Deanna Harms DF: Greteman Group
Telegraph Center

front

MAHA YOGA (USA)
CD, AD, D: Petrula Vrontikis DF: Vrontikis Design Office *Yoga Studio*

back

MAHA YOGA (USA)

front

HOTEL AT OLDTOWN (USA)
CD, AD: Sonia Greteman AD, D: James Strange DF: Greteman Group *Hotel*

back

HOTEL AT OLDTOWN (USA)

HANDMADE COLLECTION (Hong Kong)
CD: Gary Tam D: Joel Ong / Alex Chan / Ivy Wong DF: Teamwork Design Ltd.
Handmade Products Maker

CLOTIA WOOD & METAL WORKS INC. (USA)
CD, AD, D, I : Sherrie & Tracy Holdeman DF: Insight Design Communications
Wood & Metal Working Firm

RECESS (USA)
CD, D: Barbara Chan DF: Barbara Chan Design
Hair Accessories Retailer

ARENA STAGE (USA)
CD, AD: Scott Mires D: Miguel Perez
DF: Mires Design, Inc. *Regional Theater*

ARENA STAGE (USA)

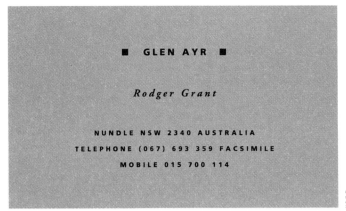

RODGER GRANT (Australia)
CD, AD, D: Sophie Bartho I: Barry Olive DF: Sophie Bartho & Associates
Cattle Grazier

RODGER GRANT (Australia)

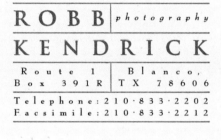

WEIS DESIGN (USA)
CD, AD, D, I: Lonnie Weis DF: Weis Design
Design Frim

ROBB KENDRICK/BAD DOG RANCH (USA)
CD, AD, D: Mark Brinkman DF: Sibley/Peteet Design
Photographer

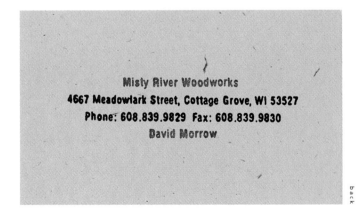

MISTY RIVER WOODWORKS (USA)
CD: Kevin Wade D: Martha Graettinger DF: Planet Design Company
Woodworking Company

MISTY RIVER WOODWORKS (USA)

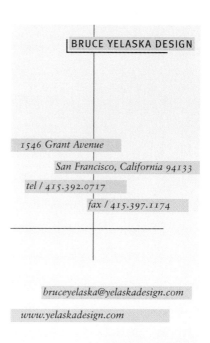

1546 Grant Avenue

San Francisco, California 94133

tel / 415.392.0717

fax / 415.397.1174

bruceyelaska@yelaskadesign.com

www.yelaskadesign.com

BRUCE YELASKA

BRUCE YELASKA DESIGN (USA)
CD, AD, D: Bruce Yelaska DF: Bruce Yelaska Design
Graphic & Product Design Company

Academy of
Chinese
Acupuncture
e.V.

front

ACADEMY OF CHINESE
ACUPUNCTURE E.V. (Germany)
D: Wladimir Perlin DF: Wladimir Perlin -
Graphic Design & Advertising
Academy

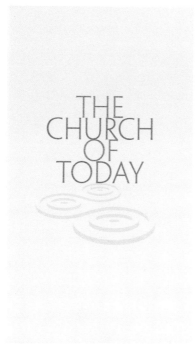

THE
CHURCH
OF
TODAY

front

THE CHURCH OF TODAY (USA)
CD, AD: Scott Mires D, I: Miguel Perez
DF: Mires Design, Inc. *Church*

HUNAN
湖南園
GARDEN

RESTAURANT | PATIO | BAR

Simon Yuan

3345 EL CAMINO REAL
PALO ALTO, CA 94306

TEL | 650.565.8868

FAX | 650.565.8818

HUNAN GARDEN RESTAURANT (USA)
CD, AD, D, I: Bruce Yelaska DF: Bruce Yelaska
Design *Restaurant*

Thomas Pfeiffer

Organisation

Ihr Ansprechpartner
für Deutschland,
Schweiz, Schweden

Jenaer Straße 16
D-10717 Berlin
Tel.: 030 / 853 96 32
Fax: 030 / 854 92 85

back

ACADEMY OF CHINESE
ACUPUNCTURE E.V. (Germany)

WENDY CRAIG-PURCELL
MINISTER AND
CHIEF EXECUTIVE OFFICER

8999 ACTIVITY ROAD

SAN DIEGO, CALIFORNIA 92126

TELEPHONE: 619-689-6500

FACSIMILE: 619-689-6505

EMAIL@CHURCHOFTODAY.ORG

WWW.CHURCHOFTODAY.ORG

A CHURCH THAT FITS YOUR LIFE

back

THE CHURCH OF TODAY (USA)

DEBRA ROBERTS

15345 VIA SIMPATICO

AND ASSOCIATES

RANCHO SANTA FE

INCORPORATED

CALIFORNIA 92091

DEBRA J. ROBERTS, CFA

TEL 619-759-2649

PRESIDENT AND CEO

FAX 619-759-2653

DEBRA ROBERTS & ASSOCIATES (USA)
CD, AD, D: Scott Mires D: Deborah Hom
DF: Mires Design, Inc.
Corporate Consultants

THE—MULTIMEDIA—WORKSHOP

front

THE MULTIMEDIA WORKSHOP (USA)
AD, D: Brett Stiles DF: GSD + M
Electronic Media Buying Service Provider

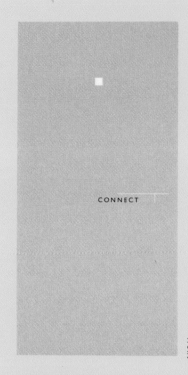

CONNECT

front

MAHLUM (USA)
AD, D: Jack Anderson D: Heidi Favour /
Margaret Long DF: Hornall Anderson
Design Works, Inc.
Architectural Design Firm

OLD

SILVER

WOOD

3F TRUCK
1-6-13, Uemachi, Chuo-ku
Osaka, 540-0005 JAPAN
TEL/FAX; 06-761-2765

Yoshihisa Mizuno

OLD SILVER WOOD (Japan)
AD: Mika Noguchi D: Yoshiko Honda DF: Miranda Co.
Accessory Retailer

TINA WILLIAMSON

TMW GROUP

3707 Counselor Drive | Austin, Texas 78749
|P| 512-292-6255 |F| 512-282-1808 | email: tina@tmw-group.com

back

THE MULTIMEDIA WORKSHOP (USA)

MAHLUM
architects

Michael L. Smith, AIA
principal

msmith@mahlum.com

1231
NW Hoyt
SUITE   102
Portland, OR
97209

503
224.4032
503
224.0918   *f*

back

MAHLUM (USA)

front

back

VERDE COMMUNICATIONS (USA)
CD, AD, D: John Ball D: Kathy Carpentier-Moore DF: Mires Design, Inc.
CD-ROM Publisher

VERDE COMMUNICATIONS (USA)

CAFFÉ @ IDÉE (Japan)
AD, D: de-ge Takuji Nomoto *Cafe*

KIM KACHOUGIAN (USA)
D: Tim Morse DF: Coloured Hard Inc. *Personal*

front

back

DES PRÉS CAFÉ (Japan)
AD, D: Takeshi Nishimura DF: Completo Inc. *Cafe*

DES PRÉS CAFÉ (Japan)

CASE (Netherlands) D: Kees Wagenaars DF: Case
Graphic Design Firm

MINIMAX (Australia)
CD, AD, D, I: Phil Ellett DF: Cozzolino Ellett Design D'Vision
Houseware Retailer

front

DICK PATRICK STUDIOS (USA)
CD, D: Mark Ford DF: Swieter Design U. S. *Photographer*

back

DICK PATRICK STUDIOS (USA)

front

STARR LITIGATION (USA)
CD, AD, D, I: John Sayles DF: Sayles Graphic Design
Litigation Service Provider

back

STARR LITIGATION (USA)

KINETIK COMMUNICATION GRAPHICS INC. (USA)
AD, D: Jeffrey Fabian / Samuel G. Shelton D: Amy Gustincic /
Mimi Masse / Scott Rier / Erin Shigaki DF: KINETIK Communication
Graphics, Inc. *Graphic Design Firm*

HORNALL ANDERSON DESIGN WORKS (USA)
AD, D: Jack Anderson D, I: David Bates DF: Hornall Anderson
Design Works, Inc. *Graphic Design Firm*

1. SABBY GENTTEEL (Japan) *Fashion Retailer*
2. FUTURE ∂ WORK (USA) CD: Ken Widmeyer D: Christopher Downs / Dale Hart DF: Widmeyer Design *Prototype Office Exhibit Company*
3. I-D BÜRO (Germany) CD, AD, D, P, I, CW: Oliver A. Krimmel / Anja Oslerwalder DF: i-d Buero *Graphic Design Firm*

WIDMEYER DESIGN (USA)
CD: Ken Widmeyer D: Brian Piper DF: Widmeyer Design
Graphic Design Firm

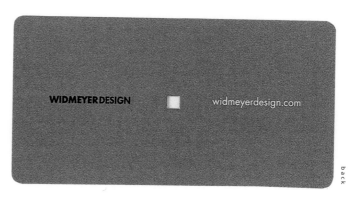

WIDMEYER DESIGN (USA)

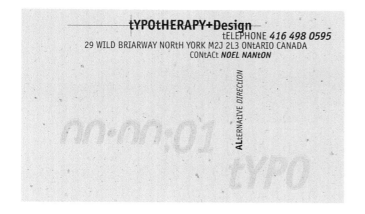

TYPOTHERAPY + DESIGN (Canada)
CD, AD, D: Noël Nanton DF: tYPOtHERAPY + DESiGN
Graphic Design Firm

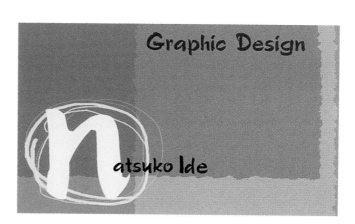

NATSUKO IDE (Japan)
D: Natsuko Ide *Graphic Designer*

GRAPHIC HAVOC AVA (USA)
CD, AD, D: Derek Lerner *Graphic Design Firm*

GRAPHIC HAVOC AVA (USA)

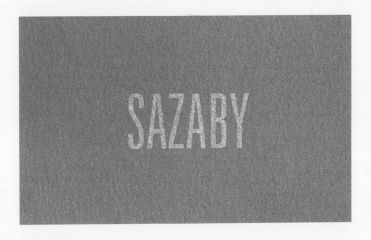

SAZABY INC. (Japan)
CD: SAZABY Inc. AD, DF: SAZABY Graphic Design D: Chie Kusakari
Interior & Fashion Goods Retailer

AIX (Japan)
CD: SAZABY Inc. AD, DF: SAZABY Graphic Design D: Hatsuko Kobayashi /
Naomi Katagiri *Fashion Retailer*

MARY GALLEA (USA)
CD, AD: Steven Sikora D: Mitch Morse DF: Design Guys
Print Production

ICL (Japan)
CD: SAZABY Inc. AD, DF: SAZABY Graphic Design D: Hatsuko Kobayashi /
Chikako Nishimura *Interior Goods & Furniture Retailer*

&A. (Japan)
CD: SAZABY Inc. AD, DF: SAZABY Graphic Design D: Chie Kusakari
Sundry Goods Retailer

1, 2. SIMON & GOETZ (Germany) CD, AD, D: Ruediger Goetz I: Elke Boehm DF: Simon & Goetz Design *Advertising Agency*
3. PERSONIFY CORPORATION (USA) AD, D: Jack Anderson D: Debra McCloskey / Holly Finlayson DF: Hornall Anderson Design Works, Inc.
   Software Manufacturer

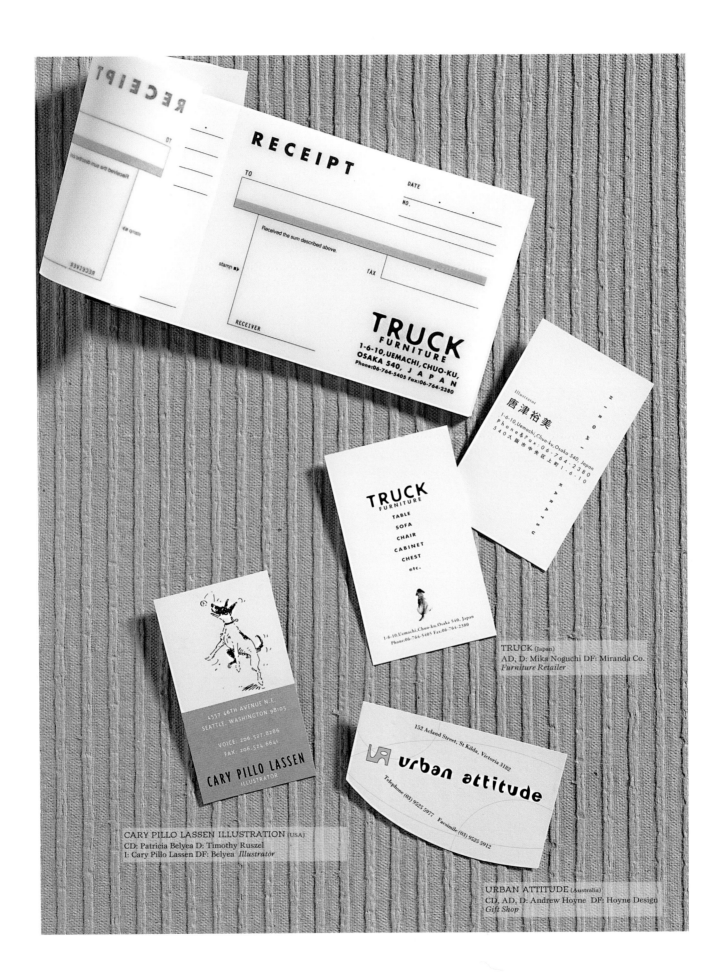

RECEIPT

RECEIPT

TO

DATE

NO.

Received the sum described above.

stamp ▪▶

FAX

RECEIVER

TRUCK
FURNITURE
1-6-10,UEMACHI, CHUO-KU,
OSAKA 540, J A P A N
Phone:06-764-5405 Fax:06-764-2380

TRUCK
FURNITURE

TABLE
SOFA
CHAIR
CABINET
CHEST
etc.

1-6-10,Uemachi,Chuo-ku,Osaka 540, Japan
Phone:06-764-5405 Fax:06-764-2380

Illustrator
唐津裕美
1-6-10.Uemachi,Chuo-ku Osaka 540, Japan
phone&Fax:06-764-2380
540 大阪市中央区上町1-6-10

N I R O M I

K A R A T S U

4557 46TH AVENUE N.E.
SEATTLE, WASHINGTON 98105

VOICE: 206.527.8286
FAX: 206.524.6641

CARY PILLO LASSEN
ILLUSTRATOR

152 Acland Street, St Kilda, Victoria 3182

urban attitude

Telephone (03) 9525 5977   Facsimile (03) 9525 5912

TRUCK (Japan)
AD; D: Mika Noguchi DF: Miranda Co.
Furniture Retailer

CARY PILLO LASSEN ILLUSTRATION (USA)
CD: Patricia Belyea D: Timothy Ruszel
I: Cary Pillo Lassen DF: Belyea *Illustrator*

URBAN ATTITUDE (Australia)
CD, AD, D: Andrew Hoyne DF: Hoyne Design
Gift Shop

CONTACT REFLEX ANALYSIS (USA) AD, D: Jeff Welsh P: Photodisc DF: Big Kid Design Club *Clinical Nutrition Company*

CHA YU ALAN CHAN TEA ROOM (Japan)
CD, D: Alan Chan *Tea Room*

CHA YU ALAN CHAN TEA ROOM (Japan)

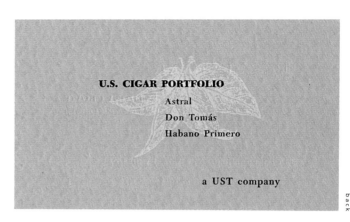

U.S. CIGAR (USA)
AD: Jack Anderson AD, D: Larry Anderson D: Mary Hermes / Mike Calkins /
Michael Brugman DF: Hornall Anderson Design Works, Inc.
Cigar Distributor

U.S. CIGAR (USA)

TOM CONNORS PHOTOGRAPHY (USA)
CD, AD, D: Michael Connors DF: Motive Design Research
Commercial Photography Studio

TOM CONNORS PHOTOGRAPHY (USA)

LUX ART INSTITUTE (USA)
CD, AD: John Ball D, I: Miguel Perez DF: Mires Design, Inc.
Art Institution

LUX ART INSTITUTE (USA)

PROCTOR BRONZES (USA)
CD, AD, D, P, I: Kari Strand DF: Motive Design Research
Art Dealer

Phimister Procter Church

PROCTOR BRONZES
8020 HANSEN ROAD NORTHEAST
BAINBRIDGE ISLAND, WASHINGTON
98110
206 | 842.2512   *fax* 206 | 842.2512
SSCHURCH@SPRYNET.COM

WWW.ALTMOTIVE.COM/PROCTOR

CIRCA-THE PRINCE (Australia)
CD, AD, D: Andrew Hoyne D: Tash Schroter
DF: Hoyne Design *Restaurant*

circa
THE PRINCE

2 Acland Street
St Kilda Melbourne 3182
Telephone 03 9536 1122
Facsmile 03 9536 1133

1. HITACHIYA-HONPO (Japan) AD: Yoshinari Hisazumi D: Tetsuya Hoshiya DF: Hisazumi Design Room *Beverage Maker*
2. DRUCKEREI WENIN OHG (Austria) AD, D: Sigi Ramoser D: Klaus Österle DF: Atelier für Text und Gestaltung *Printing Company*
3. BRENT HUMPHREYS (USA) CD, D: Mark Ford DF: Swieter Design U. S. *Photographer*
4. INSURANCE MARKETPLACE (USA) CD: Rex Peteet AD, D, I: Mark Brinkman DF: Sibley/Peteet Design *Insurance Company*

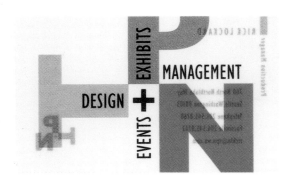

THE PRODUCTION NETWORK (USA)
CD: Ken Widmeyer D: Dale Hart / Tony Secolo DF: Widmeyer Design
Event Designers

PARENTS ANONYMOUS OF TEXAS (USA)
AD, D: Brett Stiles DF: GSD + M
Non-Profit Company to Prevent Child Abuse

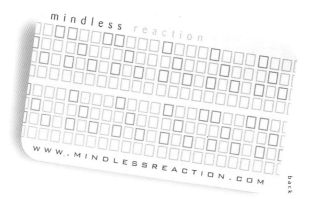

MINDLESS REACTION (USA) CD: Joven Orozco D: Brandon Mercado DF: Joven Orozco Design *Apparel Maker*

MAMA RECORDS (USA)
CD, AD: Petrula Vrontikis D: Victor Corpuz / Winnie Li DF: Vrontikis
Design Office *Record Lablel*

ROSLYN ESKIND ASSOCIATES LIMITED (Canada)
CD, AD, D, CW: Roslyn Eskind DF: Roslyn Eskind Associates Limited
Graphic Design Firm

back 1

KAZUNORI SADAHIRO (Japan)
D, I: Kazunori Sadahiro *Designer & Illustrator*

☒ イラスト ☒ デザイン ☒ ペインティング

s

〒185-0036 東京都 国分寺市 高木町 3-6-2
メゾン・ド・ニレ #102 サダヒロカズノリ 図案室
電話 042-575-3664 ■
ファクシミリ 042-575-3664 ■
sadahiro@din.or.jp

サ ダ ヒ ロ カズ ノリ

front

KAZUNORI SADAHIRO (Japan)

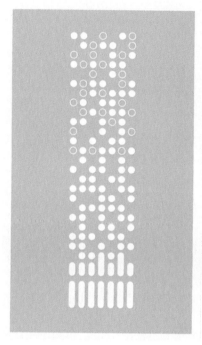

back 2

KAZUNORI SADAHIRO (Japan)

cafe

shayne farquhar

p 9866 5239

m 0419 340 309

f 9866 5875

e cafehead@ozramp.net.au

a 314 Punt Road. South Yarra. Vic. 3141

ADVERTISING

CAFE ADVERTISING (Australia)
AD, D: Saskia Ericson DF: SAS Art *Advertising & Marketing Consultancy*

michael BARTALOS **p** 415 863 4569 **f** 415 252 7252
mike@bartalos.com

30 RAMONA AVENUE NO.2 SAN FRANCISCO CA 94103

represented in japan by **CWC**
p 03 3496 0745 **f** 03 3496 0747 **e** junko@cwctokyo.com

MICHAEL BARTALOS (USA)
I: Michael Bartalos *Illustrator*

axis technologies LLC 7683 southeast 27th number 303

mercer island, washington 98040 tel 206.236.0336 fax 206.236.0369

rballen@axistechnologies.com www.axistechnologies.com

RON BALLEN

AXIS

front

back

AXIS TECHNOLOGIES (USA)
CD: Ken Widmeyer D: Dale Hart DF: Widmeyer Design
Computer Company

AXIS TECHNOLOGIES (USA)

phone 315 449 2092
fax 315 449 0896

Don Carr

CARR&LAMB DESIGN

339 SCOTT AVENUE,
SYRACUSE, NEW YORK 13224
CARR2LAMB@AOL.COM

CARR & LAMB DESIGN (USA)
CD, AD, D, I: Denise Heckman DF: Motive Design Research
Design Firm

GEOFFREY VEIVERS

GENERAL MANAGER

MARKPATRICKAGENCY

LEVEL 1, 17 KNOX LANE DOUBLE BAY NSW AUSTRALIA 2028

TELEPHONE 61 2 363 0311 FACSIMILE 61 2 363 0361

front

back

MARK PATRICK AGENCY (Australia)
CD, AD, D: Sophie Bartho DF: Sophie Bartho & Associates
Marketing & PR Company

MARK PATRICK AGENCY (Australia)

DESIGN STUDIO BLUE-? (Japan)
AD, D: Koichi Shoji   D: Takamasa Hatsuda DF: design studio BLUE-?
Graphic Design Firm

CROSS WORLD CONNECTIONS (CWC) (Japan)
Logo Designer: Isabelle Dervaux
Creative Agency

KID BLUE CO. LTD. (Japan)
D: Isao Shimogama *Inner-Wear Retailer*

He that hath two cakes of bread, let him sell
one of them and buy Narcissus, for bread is food
for the body but Narcissus is food for the soul,

F.O.B COOP

He that hath two cakes
of bread, let him sell one
of them and buy Narciss-
us, for bread is food for the
body but Narcissus is food
for the soul,

F.O.B CO-OP
HARAJUKU

F.O.B CO-OP (Japan)
CD: Mitue Masunaga D: Yumi Takahashi
Interior Goods Retailer

KIWAKO INAMORI (Japan)
AD, D: Shigeru Kanematsu DF: O-Five Remix *Writer*

AZUSA KOTAKE (Japan)
AD, D: Shigeru Kanematsu DF: O-Five Remix *Model*

MAKIKO NIWA (Japan)
AD, D: Shigeru Kanematsu DF: O-Five Remix *Writer*

MASUMI KADOSHIMA (Japan)
AD, D: Shigeru Kanematsu DF: O-Five Remix *Planner & Editor*

CHICA SAWADA (Japan)
AD, D: Shigeru Kanematsu DF: O-Five Remix
Hair & Make-up Artist

TRIBUTE & CO (Japan)
AD, D: Michio Iijima DF: O-Five Remix *Editorial*
Planning Company

MILLENNIUM
RESTAURANT
CONSULTANTS

TOM DUFFY
PRESIDENT

15700 GUM TREE LANE
LOS GATOS, CA 95032

TEL: 415.971.9191
TEL: 408.358.9697

FAX: 650.375.8313
FAX: 408.358.9653

front

MILLENNIUM RESTAURANT
CONSULTANTS (USA)

back

MILLENNIUM RESTAURANT CONSULTANTS (USA)
CD, AD, D: Bruce Yelaska P: Kelly Low DF: Bruce Yelaska Design
Restaurant Consultants

OLIVER ELTINGER

kronprinzenstraße 108
40217 düsseldorf
fon 0211.34 02 39
fax 0211.3 19 04 84

fotografie

OLIVER ELTINGER (Germany)
AD, D: Fons M. Hickmann DF: Fons M. Hickmann Design
Photographer

BIKRAM'S

COLLEGE

OF INDIA

1816 Magnolia Ave.
Burlingame, CA 94010
Tel: 650.552.9642 (YOGA)
www.bikramyoga.com

ROBIN SCHMIDT (USA)
CD, AD, D: Bruce Yelaska DF: Bruce Yelaska Design
Yoga School

ᴜɴɪᴄᴏᴍ

Unicom
System Engineering Company

Tel 2690 0789   Fax 2690 0997   **Mobile** 8107 9777
Flat 18, 6th Floor Wah Yiu Industrial Building
30-32 Au Pui Wan Street
Fo Tan, Shatin, N.T., Hong Kong

front

UNICOM SYSTEM ENGINEERING COMPANY (Hong Kong)
AD: Gabriel Tsang D: Iris Kwok DF: Tupos Design Company
Engineering Company

back

UNICOM SYSTEM ENGINEERING COMPANY (Hong Kong)

Toni Schowalter Design

TS

Toni Schowalter Design

Graphic

Communications

kim
reg. massage therapist

swedish
sports-orthopedics
geriatrics
pediatrics
stress management
office seated
on-site massage

No.

DENISE FORD   Agent
5114 Milam Dallas, Texas 75206

tel 214 821 6788   fax 821 0566

TONI SCHOWALTER DESIGN (USA)
CD, AD, D: Toni Schowalter DF: Toni Schowalter Design
Graphic Design Firm

DENISE FORT, AGENT (USA)
CD, D: Mark Ford DF: Swieter Design U. S.
Photographers' Agent

KIM FORD (USA)
CD, D: Mark Ford DF: Swieter Design U. S.
Registered Massage Agent

LENZ BEREUTER (Austria)
CD, AD, D: Sigi Ramoser CD: Sandro Scherling AD: Klaus Österle
DF: Atelier für Text und Gestaltung *Tax Consultancy*

President
TAKAHIKO MIZUNO

HIKO·MIZUNO COLLEGE OF JEWELRY
5-29-2, JINGUMAE, SHIBUYA-KU
TOKYO, 150 JAPAN
TEL.03-3499-0300 FAX.03-3499-0343
FAX.(DIRECT) 03-3499-0309

HIKO MIZUNO COLLEGE OF JEWELRY (Japan)
CD, AD, D: Zempaku Suzuki DF: BBI Studio Inc. *College*

198 Mary Street
Richmond 3121 Victoria
Telephone: 03 9429 9888
Facsimile: 03 9429 9877
e-mail: Info@Metalicus.com
HTTP://WWW.Metalicus.com

METALICUS AUSTRALIA (Australia)
CD, AD: Andrew Hoyne D: Rachel Miles DF: Hoyne Design
Apparel Maker

CONCIERGE (Japan)
CD, AD: Takahisa Kamiya *Fashion Goods Retailer*

MALCOLM MCGREGOR
PURCHASING MANAGER
mmcgregor@protix.com

PROTIX POINT-OF-SALE GROUP
14 STRAWBERRY HILL AVE
NORWALK, CT 06855
PH: 203.831.6616
FX: 203.831.6618
WEB: www.protix.com

PROTIX (USA)
CD: Dana Lytle D: Jamie Karlin DF: Planet Design Company
Ticketing Software Company

06 6245 1105

3f, 1-16-9, Higashishinsaibashi, Chuo-ku, Osaka, Japan 542-0083

SALON DE MABU

SALON DE MABU (Japan)
AD, D: Mika Noguchi DF: Miranda Co. *Beauty Salon*

ROTONDA
SUL MARE

487 SEAPORT COURT • REDWOOD CITY, CA 94063
TEL 415-306-0862 • FAX 415-306-0866

ROGER DIOLI

LA ROTONDA SUL MARE (USA)
CD, AD, D: Bruce Yelaska DF: Bruce Yelaska Design *Restaurant*

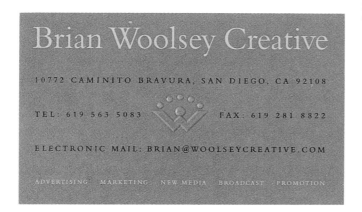

Brian Woolsey Creative

10772 CAMINITO BRAVURA, SAN DIEGO, CA 92108

TEL: 619 563 5083   FAX: 619 281 8822

ELECTRONIC MAIL: BRIAN@WOOLSEYCREATIVE.COM

ADVERTISING   MARKETING   NEW MEDIA   BROADCAST   PROMOTION

BRIAN WOOLSEY (USA)
CD, AD: Scott Mires D, I: Miguel Perez DF: Mires Design, Inc.
Professional Copywriting Service Company

Pierre Chaubert

Geigenbaumeister

im Aschenbrennerhaus
Hutergasse 2
D-87629 Füssen
Telefon 08362 921084
Fax 08362 921085

PIERRE CHAUBERT (Germany)
D: Reinhard Raich *Violin Maker*

tracy english | dyanna moon
214 stewart street seattle, wa 98101
TEL: 206-443-9660 • **FAX:** 206-443-9655

MISKITO COAST
VENTURES INC.

Cecilia de la Rocha
*Vice President Marketing
& Development*

c/o #308-165 3rd Avenue S.
Saskatoon, Saskatchewan
S7K 1L8 Canada
P. (306) 653-8835
F. (306) 653-8845
www.miskitocoast.com

MARCIA WALDORF
Partner

P.O. BOX 771
52965 CEDAR CREST ROAD
IDYLLWILD, CA 92549
PHONE: 909.659.2580
FAX: 909.659.3700
EMAIL: WINPROD@AOL.COM

stellaBEAM

STELLA BEAM BOUTIQUE (USA)
D: Karen Cheng DF: Happy Design
Boutique

MISKITO COAST VENTURES (Canada)
CD, AD: Catharine Bradbury D: Dean Bartsch
DF: Bradbury Design Inc.
Management Consultants

WALDORF CRAWFORD (USA)
CD, AD: Stan Evenson D: Mark Sojka
DF: Evenson Design Group *Marketing &
Communications Firm*

Lori L. Leseberg, CPA
Controller

■

2673 NE University Village,
Suite 7
Seattle, Washington
98105

206-523-0622
Fax 206-525-3859
E-mail: lorill@ix.netcom.com

Charlottesville, VA
Phone 804-964-1575
Fax 804-964-1345
valmontis@comclin.net

THETYPINGPOOL

Morag Urquhart

SECURITY HOUSE 68-70 DUNDAS COURT
PHILLIP CANBERRA ACT 2606

PHONE (06)281 5452   FAX (06)285 4544

UNIVERSITY VILLAGE (USA)
AD, D: Jack Anderson D, I: David Bates
DF: Hornall Anderson Design Works, Inc.
Retail Shopping Complex

VALMONTIS BED + BREAKFAST (USA)
CD, AD, D, P, I: Trudy Cole-Zielanski
DF: Trudy Cole-Zielanski Design
Bed & Breakfast

THE TYPING POOL (Australia)
CD, AD, D: Linda Fu DF: Linda Fu Design
Typing Service Company

EDG (USA)
CD, AD: Stan Evenson D: Amy Hershman DF: Evenson Design Group
Graphic Design Firm

STUDIO MÖBIUS (Japan)
AD, D: Misa Awatsuji DF: Awatsuji Design
Interior Design Office

SYNECTICS INTERNATIONAL (USA)
CD: John Swieter CD, D: Mark Ford DF: Swieter Design U. S.
Systems Integrators

SYNECTICS INTERNATIONAL (USA)

AWATSUJI DESIGN (Japan)
AD, D: Misa Awatsuji DF: Awatsuji Design
Design Firm

AWATSUJI DESIGN (Japan)

C is for Communication

2180 Sterling Avenue
Menlo Park, CA 94025
Anne Vitullo   tel: 650.854.2663
fax: 650.854.7926
e-mail: c_anne@worldnet.att.net

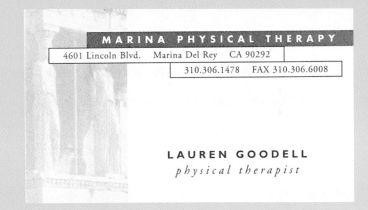

MARINA PHYSICAL THERAPY

4601 Lincoln Blvd.   Marina Del Rey   CA 90292

310.306.1478   FAX 310.306.6008

LAUREN GOODELL
physical therapist

C IS FOR COMMUNICATION (USA)
CD, AD: Stan Evenson D: Raul Ramirez DF: Evenson Design Group
Marketing & Communications Firm

MARINA PHYSICAL THERAPY (USA)
CD, AD: Stan Evenson D: Euwook Chung DF: Evenson Design Group *Hospital*

THE
GAUNTLETT
GROUP

Elizabeth Renshaw
Research & Marketing Coordinator
Direct: 415.882.5318

901 Market Street, Suite 440
San Francisco, CA 94103
Tel: 415.882.5310
Fax: 415.882.5319
E-mail: erenshaw@gauntlettgroup.com

Helping Companies Profit from Environmental Performance

DONNELLEY
ENTERPRISE
SOLUTIONS
INCORPORATED

Systems Management Group
DAVID J. SHEA
Senior Vice President/General Manager

NINETY-NINE PARK AVENUE
NEW YORK, NY 10016-1510
TEL: 212 503 1457 FAX: 212 503 8648
E MAIL: d s h e a @ d e s i . n e t

THE GAUNTLETT GROUP (USA)
CD, AD, D: Bruce Yelaska DF: Bruce Yelaska Design
Environmental Engineering Firm

DONNELLEY ENTERPRISE SOLUTIONS (USA)
CD, AD, D: Jose A. Serrano D: Miguel Perez DF: Mires Design, Inc.
Information Management Services Company

FOSTER PEPPER & SHEFELMAN
A PROFESSIONAL LIMITED LIABILITY COMPANY

LYNNE E. GRAYBEAL
Attorney at Law

Direct Phone
(206)447-2892
Direct Facsimile
(206)749-1948

IIII THIRD
AVENUE
Suite 3400
SEATTLE
Washington
98101-3299

E-mail
GRAYL@FOSTER.COM
Website
WWW.FOSTER.COM

FOSTER HART
L A W Y E R S

Cameron Abbott B.Com., LL.B. (Hons.)
Senior Associate

Level 14 565 Bourke Street
Melbourne VIC 3000
GPO Box 1193K Melbourne 3001
DX 549 Melbourne
Telephone (03) 9620 1000
Direct Line (03) 9612 2005
Facsimile (03) 9620 5585
Email lawyers@fosterhart.com.au

FOSTER PEPPER SHEFELMAN (USA)
AD, D: John Hornall D: Katha Dalton / Nicole Bloss / Julie Keenan Calligrapher: Dia
Calhonn DF: Hornall Anderson Design Works, Inc. *Law Firm*

FOSTER HART (Australia)
CD, AD, D: Andrew Hoyne DF: Hoyne Design
Law Firm

ENGBERG ANDERSON (USA)
CD: Kevin Wade D: Martha Graettinger DF: Planet Design Company
Architects

ENGBERG ANDERSON (USA)

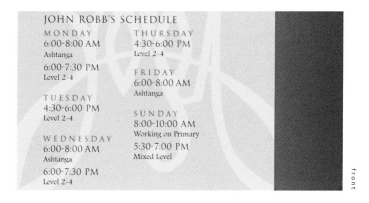

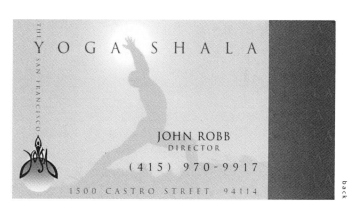

YOGA SHALA / JOHN ROBB (USA)
CD, AD, D: Petrula Vrontikis D: Susan Carter DF: Vrontikis Design Office
Yoga Studio

YOGA SHALA / JOHN ROBB (USA)

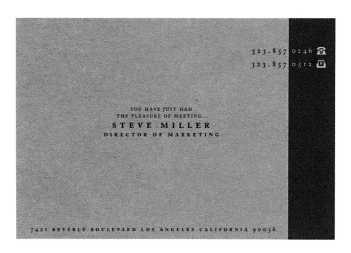

ATELIER LE SYMBOLE (Netherlands)
CD: Arno Bauman D: Marco Stout DF: Studio Bauman BNO
Gold & Silversmith

138 DEGREES (USA)
CD: Peter Bureba AD: Martyn Atkins D: Steven Murashige DF: 138 Degrees
Design Firm

ADAMS OUTDOOR ADVERTISING (USA)
CD: Kevin Wade D: Martha Graettinger
DF: Planet Design Company
Outdoor Advertising Firm

GIFT STATION (Taiwan)
AD, D: Billy Chang DF: Gift Station
Gift Design Company

JAYSON HAIT / EYE 4 DETAIL (USA)
AD, D: Jeffrey Fabian / Samuel G. Shelton D: Henry Quiroga /
Scott Rier DF: KINETIK Communication Graphics, Inc.
Editor & Writer

JABRA CORPORATION (USA)
CD, AD: Scott Mires D, I: Miguel Perez DF: Mires Design, Inc.
Industrial Manufacturer

BILL ARMSTRONG COMMUNICATIONS (Canada)
CD, AD, D: Catharine Bradbury DF: Bradbury Design Inc.
Writer

SALON POMPEO (USA)
CD, D: Mark Ford DF: Swieter Design U.S.
Beauty Salon

HENNING WAGNER (Germany)
AD, D: Fons M. Hickmann DF: Fons M. Hickmann Design
Dentist

WINGS OF DESIRE (Australia)
CD, AD, D: Saskia Ericson DF: SAS Art
Travel Agency

SARA BERGINC (Slovenia)
AD, D: Edi Berk DF: KROG *Personal*

BARBARA CHAN DESIGN (USA)
CD, D: Barbara Chan DF: Barbara Chan Design
Graphic Design Firm

INTERNATIONAL DINING ADVENTURES (USA)
CD: Patricia Belyea D, I: Christian Salas DF: Belyea
Travel Company

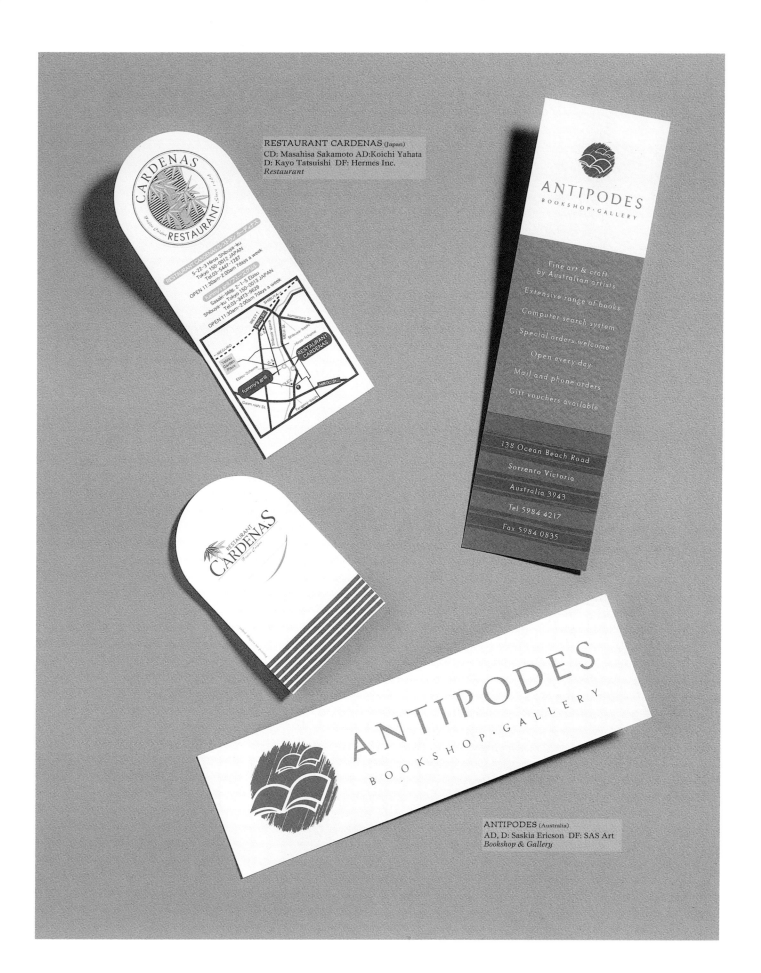

RESTAURANT CARDENAS (Japan)
CD: Masahisa Sakamoto AD:Koichi Yahata
D: Kayo Tatsuishi DF: Hermes Inc.
Restaurant

ANTIPODES (Australia)
AD, D: Saskia Ericson DF: SAS Art
Bookshop & Gallery

STUDIO ORANGE (UK)
AD, D: Yuki Miyake DF: System Gafa
Furniture & Interior Designer

COMPLETO INC. (Japan)
AD, D: Takeshi Nishimura DF: Completo Inc.
Graphic Design Firm

TRAX INC. (Japan)
AD, D: Michio Miura DF: trax Inc.
Advertising Production

KIRAKIRA (Japan)
AD, D: Masahiro Matsushige CW: Hifumi Harima DF: KIRAKIRA
Editorial & Design Firm

ECLECTICA (Netherlands)
CD, D: Arno Bauman DF: Studio Bauman BNO
Coaching, Training & Communication Advisor

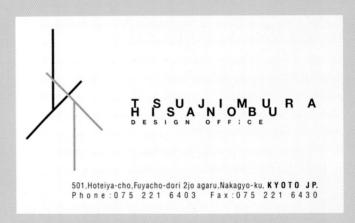

TSUJIMURA HISANOBU DESIGN OFFICE (JAPAN)
AD, D: Mika Noguchi DF: Miranda Co.
Architecture & Interior Design Firm

JUNICHI MORI
PRESIDENT

tokyo
3 · 5 · 3 YOYOGI
SHIBUYA · KU
TOKYO 151-0053
● 03 · 5351 · 7087
● 03 · 5351 · 4744

london
FLAT3 97 · C
KENSINGTON
CHURCH ST
LONDON W8 7LN
● 171 · 221 · 8156

● ALSUR

ALSUR CO., LTD. (Japan)
CD, AD, D: Tabito Mizuo
Fashion Wholesaler

Ann Gusiff

Executive Director

Clothes The Deal
1666 Whitefield Road
Pasadena, CA 91104
(818) 798-9186
(818) 798-9187 Fax.

CLOTHES THE DEAL

CLOTHES THE DEAL (USA)
CD, D: Mamoru Shimokochi D: Anne Reeves DF: Shimokochi/Reeves
Non-Profit Organization

5959 Peacock Ridge Rd., #6
Rancho Palos Verdes, CA 90274
Phone: 310 541 3587
Fax: 310 541 8617

IZEN (USA)
CD, D: Mamoru Shimokochi D: Anne Reeves DF: Shimokochi/Reeves
Textile Designer

SHAMUS GONELLA

WRITER / JOURNALIST

WORDS ● ALIVE

PO BOX 1803 WODEN CANBERRA ACT 2606

PHONE/FAX (06) 287 3037   MOBILE 0411 466 686

WORDS ALIVE (Australia)
CD, D: Linda Fu DF: Linda Fu Design
Creative Writing Company

F o r s y t h e

d e s i g n

www.forsythedesign.com

142 Berkeley Street, 4th Floor
Boston, MA 02116

t 617 437 1023
f 617 437 1143

Kathleen Forsythe kf@forsythedesign.com

information, graphic + new media design

FORSYTHE DESIGN (USA)
AD: Kathleen Forsythe D: Shannon Beer DF: Forsythe Design
Graphic Design Firm

KELLY GRAHAM
Marketing Director

Crystal
mountain

33914 Crystal Mtn. Blvd.
Crystal Mountain WA 98022
FAX 360.663.0148
TEL 360.663.2265
A Boyne USA Resort

1

Texas Health Care
Information Council

Nghia Quan
Systems Analyst

Telephone: 512 424-6407
Facsimile: 512 424-6491
nquan@thcic.state.tx.us
www.thcic.state.tx.us
4900 N Lamar, Suite 3407
Austin, Texas 78751-2399

2

Ancient Mariner Productions
A STEPPINGSTONE COMPANY

2216 River Hills Road, Suite A
Austin, Texas 78733

Telephone: 512.263.7
Facsimile: 512.263
E-mail: steppingston

John Bernardoni
EXECUTIVE PRODUCER

ANCIENT
MARINER

3

Charles Breed
Sr. Director
Technical Marketing

PRETTY GOOD PRIVACY

2121 S. El Camino Real
San Mateo, CA 94403
Voice: 415.572.0430
Fax: 415.572.1932

Direct: 415.524.6221
Web: www.pgp.com
Email: cbreed@pgp.com

4

1. CRYSTAL MOUNTAIN RESORT (USA) CD: Ken Widmeyer D: Dale Hart DF: Widmeyer Design *Recreatinal Resort*
2. TEXAS HEALTH CARE INFORMATION COUNCIL (USA) CD, AD, D, I: Mark Brinkman D, I: Julie Berend DF: Sibley/Peteet Design
   Health Care Infomation Providers
3. ANCIENT MARINER (USA) CD, AD, D, I: Rex Peteet DF: Sibley/Peteet Design *Concert & Special Event Promoter*
4. PGP (USA) AD, D: Jack Anderson D: Debra McCloskey / Heidi Favour DF: Hornall Anderson Design Works, Inc. *Software Company*

1. CF2GS (USA) AD, D: Jack Anderson D: David Bates DF: Hornall Anderson Design Works, Inc. *Public Relations Firm*
2. TRUNK (Japan) CD, AD, D: Shinji Tanase DF: Grandcanyon Entertainment Inc. *Photography Studio*
3. AVENUE ONE PROPERTIES (USA) CD, AD, I: Rex Peteet AD, D: Matt Heck D: Ty Taylor DF: Sibley/Peteet Design *Real Estate Firm*

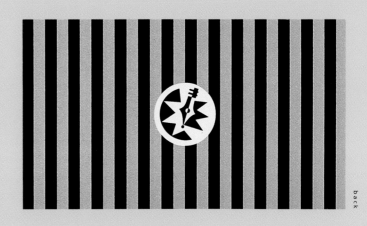

LABRUE COMMUNICATIONS (USA)
CD, D: Greg Walters DF: Greg Walters Design
Marketing Communications Firm

LABRUE COMMUNICATIONS (USA)

SCOTT STOLL PHOTOGRAPHY (USA)
CD: Patricia Belyea D, I: Christian Salas DF: Belyea
Photographer

ANACOMP (USA)
CD, AD: John Ball D: Miguel Perez DF: Mires Design, Inc.
Industrial & Manufacturing Company

SURFACE DESIGN (USA)

SURFACE DESIGN (USA) CD, D: Greg Walters DF: Greg Walters Design
Interior Surface Painter

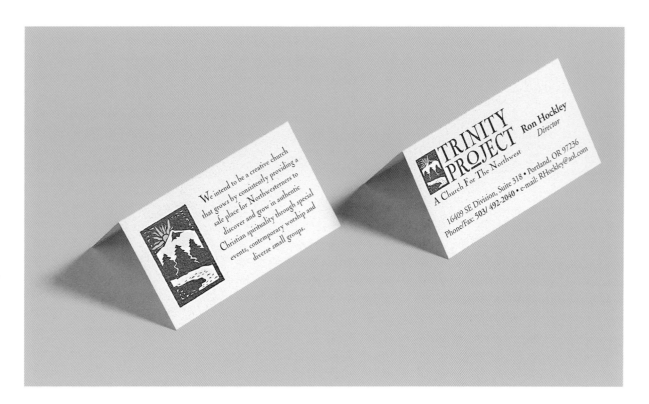

TRINITY PROJECT (USA) CD, AD, D, I: Jeff Fisher DF: Jeff Fisher LogoMotives *Church*

MARKUS WOHLGENANNT (Austria) D: Sigi Ramoser / Klaus Österle CW: Elke Burtscher DF: Atelier für Text und Gestaltung *Furniture Maker*

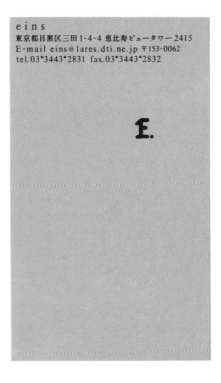

eins
東京都目黒区三田1-4-4 恵比寿ビュータワー 2415
E-mail eins@lares.dti.ne.jp 〒153-0062
tel.03*3443*2831 fax.03*3443*2832

£.

UNITED TEACHERS OF WICHITA (USA)
CD, AD: Sonia Greteman AD, D: James Strange DF: Greteman Group
Organization

EINS (Japan)
AD, D: Masahiro Kakinokihara DF: Draft Co., Ltd.
Typesetting Firm

NORTH TEXAS SPEECH SERVICES (USA)
CD, AD, D, DF: Stephen Zhang
Speech Therapy

INDUSTRY FILMS

LUIS KURI | director

front

260 KING ST. EAST STE. 200 TORONTO ON M5A 4L5 CANADA
T (416) 815 1717 F (416) 815 0147 shoot@industryfilms.com

back

INDUSTRY FILMS (Canada)
CD, AD, D: Vanessa Eckstein DF: Blok Design
Film Production Company

INDUSTRY FILMS (Canada)

■大阪市西成区山王1-9-3-502　TEL 06-644-3267　FAX 06-644-3268

肥田
慶子

大阪市西成区山王1-9-3-502
TEL 06-644-3267　FAX 06-644-3268

会議通訳　肥田慶子

KEIKO HIDA (Japan)
CD, AD, D: Kazunobu Kitakoga DF: Medio Inc.
Conference Interpreter

KEIKO HIDA (Japan)

有限会社 野津事務所

造形部主任

伊 藤 卓 義
TAKUYOSHI ITOU

事務所 〒197-0831 東京都あきる野市引田773-3　TEL 042-558-5400 FAX 042-558-5401
アトリエ 〒190-0013 東京都立川市富士見町2-32-27 石田産業倉庫No.5　TEL-FAX 042-525-3107

NOTSU INC. (Japan)
CD: Toshifumi Urata D: Takuyoshi Itou
Object Design Production

山 本 哲 次
TETSUJI YAMAMOTO

山 本 哲 次 デ ザ イ ン 室

Office : 135-0034 江東区永代2-31-5 内田ビル4F
　　　　 Tel.03-3643-9807／Fax.03-3643-9808
Atelier : 272-0131市川市湊16-7 第一水野ハイツ201
　　　　 Tel.047-356-3176／Fax.047-356-3176

front

back

TETSUJI YAMAMOTO DESIGN ROOM (Japan)
CD, AD: Tetsuji Yamamoto D: Sachiko Terajima DF: Tetsuji Yamamoto Design Office
Graphic Design Firm

TETSUJI YAMAMOTO DESIGN ROOM (Japan)

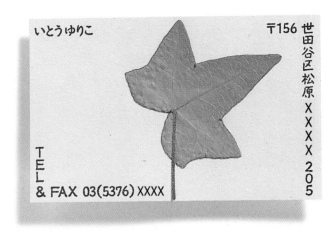

1

4

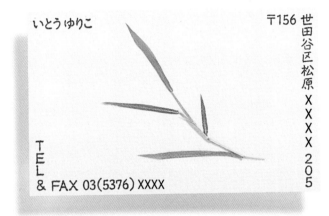

2

3

5

1,2,3, YURIKO ITOH (Japan)
D: Yuriko Itoh *Graphic Designer & Crafts Artist*

4,5, JYO-ON SEYA (Japan)
D: Yuriko Itoh
Flower Arrangement Specialist

YOSHIKO KAWAKAMI (Japan)
D: Yuriko Itoh *Editor & Writer*

YOSHIKO KAWAKAMI (Japan)

YURIKO ITOH (Japan)
D: Yuriko Itoh *Graphic Designer & Crafts Artist*

YURIKO ITOH (Japan)

F INC. (Japan)
AD: Fusashi Hagihara D: Akihiko Tsukamoto
DF: Design Club *Design Firm*

代表／ディレクター
萩原 房史

Fusashi Hagihara
President／Director

NAOI Bldg. 402, 5-47-10 Jingumae,
Shibuya-ku, Tokyo 150 Japan
Telephone (03)5466-1834
Facsimile (03)5466-1835

F INC.
Fundamental Design
is intimately bound up with
the basic business of
living our lives.

MODERN ANIMAL DESIGN (Japan)
D: Masami Nagai *Pet Goods Retailer*

永井　正己
Masami　Nagai
MODERN.ANIMAL.DESIGN.
〒152-0022東京都目黒区柿の木坂2-26-13
2-26-13,Kakinoki,zaka,Meguro-ku,tokyo,152-0022
Tel = 03-5701-6147 Fax = 03-5701-6148
E-mail = m-a-d-@t3.rim.or.jp
Url = http://www.rim.or.jp/~m-a-d-

Photographer

三島　浩

Phone・Fax 03-3463-3027

AGENT
GODO CORPORATION
176 東京都練馬区桜台4-7-11
Phone 03-3557-2958 Fax 03-3557-3596

HIROSHI MISHIMA (Japan)
AD, D: Akihiko Tsukamoto DF: Design Club
Photographer

TAKAAKI KIHARA (Japan)
D: Takaaki Kihara *Architectural Designer*

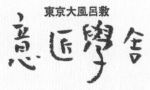

東京大風呂敷

意匠學舎

高橋 直裕

〒157 世田谷区砧公園1-2 世田谷美術館内
TEL 3415-6011　FAX3415-6413

TOKYO-OOFUROSHIKI ISHOUGAKUSHA (Japan)
D: Yuriko Itoh　Calligrapher: Naohiro Takahashi
Workshop Planner

心撮仕事人　PHOTOGRAPHER

大畑 信孝

〒547-0046　大阪市平野区平野宮町1-8-3-368
TEL/FAX 06-796-5246　HP/090-1596-9818

NOBU (Japan)
D: Shigeyo Taniguchi　*Photographer*

PHOTOGRAPHER
Nobutaka
Ohata

〒547-0046
1-8-3-368,hiranomiyamachi,hirano-ku,osaka
TEL/FAX 06-796-5246　HP/090-1596-9818

NOBU (Japan)
D: Shigeyo Taniguchi　*Photographer*

平野　雅彦

MASAHIKO HIRANO (Japan)
CD, AD, D, I: Masahiko Hirano　*Advertising Planner*

瀧本靖夫

瀧本屋

〒534-0023　大阪市都島区南通2-2-23
HP/090-1670-1773

TAKIMOTOYA (Japan)
D, I: Shigeyo Taniguchi　*Event Production*

永田俊行

Toshiyuki Nagata
Manasing Artisan

有限会社高市永光印章堂
岐阜市徹明通4-1
Telephone 058.262.6619
Facsimile 058.263.9251

各務原市那加新那加町5-5
Telephone & Facsimile 0583.71.8017

TAKAICHI EIKO INSHODO CO., LTD. (Japan)
CD, AD, D: Shinji Tanase DF: Grandcanyon Entertainment Inc.
Seal & Stamp Retailer

企画開発課
藤井 由紀

株式会社 包む
名古屋支社 〒466-0058
名古屋市昭和区白金2-9-16 TEL.052-883-3611 FAX.052-883-3616

TSUTSUMU COMPANY LIMITED (Japan)
CD: Koji Sumoto D. Yuki Fujii *Wrapping Product Maher & Retailer*

書作品
和風デザイン文字
承り処

北九州市小倉南区上石田
四・十二・二 〒八〇二

tel+fax 093-963-2718 ｜ phs 050-195-6214

front

ICHIE (Japan)
D: Hiroyuki Matsuishi *Japanese Calligrapher*

back

ICHIE (Japan)

BAR and Snack
バイキン

恩田光
ON DA KO

〒106-0031 東京都港区西麻布4-19-9
ウォール西麻布 B1
TEL 03-5469-1591・1961

BAIKIN (Japan)
AD: Keisuke Nagatomo D: Yutaka Koyama DF: K② *Restaurant*

economist
financial planner

katumi ichinose

市野瀬トータルコンサルタント
〒577-0823 東大阪市金岡3-1-7

ICHINOSE TOTAL CONSULTANT
3-1-7 Kanaoka Higashi-osaka
Japan Zip577-0823

Handy phone
090-1591-4665

Telephone   Facsimile
06-6729-5753   06-6729-5754

E-mail : ichinose@mvd.biglobe.ne.jp

KATUMI ICHINOSE (Japan)
AD, D: Yoshihide Tano DF: Mother Design Office *Economist & Financial Planner*

KAKURENBO (Japan)
D: Hitoshi Kurosaki DF: Creative Planning *Bar*

AYA SUGIYAMA (Japan)
AD, D: Kyoten Kimura DF: Rakuten Design Room
Restaurant

SUEHIRO SHOKUDO (Japan)
AD: Hitoshi Kurosaki D: Yasunori Tetsuka DF: Creative Planning
Restaurant

BAR RENGYO (Japan)
CD: Shingo Iida D: Kayo Tatsuishi Calligraphy: Izan Sakamoto DF: HERMES Inc.
Bar

SUSHI ZEN (Japan)
AD, D: Sumihiro Takeuchi DF: Sumihiro Takeuchi
Design Office *Restaurant*

Rakuten Design Room
#202, 520, Kawashima-cho, Hodogaya-ku, Yokohama-city, 240 Tel. Fax.045(373)6308
楽天デザイン室 横浜市保土ヶ谷区川島町520 サンロイヤル202

1

Rakuten Design Room
#202, 520, Kawashima-cho, Hodogaya-ku, Yokohama-city, 240 Tel. Fax.045(373)6308
楽天デザイン室 横浜市保土ヶ谷区川島町520 サンロイヤル202

2

1,2,3,4, RAKUTEN DESIGN ROOM (Japan)
AD, D: Kyoton Kimura DF: Rakuten Design Room *Graphic Design Firm*

Rakuten Design Room
#202, 520, Kawashima-cho, Hodogaya-ku, Yokohama-city, 240 Tel. Fax.045(373)6308
楽天デザイン室 横浜市保土ヶ谷区川島町520 サンロイヤル202

3

Rakuten Design Room
#202, 520, Kawashima-cho, Hodogaya-ku, Yokohama-city, 240 Tel. Fax.045(373)6308
楽天デザイン室 横浜市保土ヶ谷区川島町520 サンロイヤル202

4

野村俊夫
〒161-0031 東京都新宿区西落合4-5-20 西落合コンパウンド302号
4-5-20-302, NISHIOCHIAI, SHINJUKU-KU, TOKYO 161-0031, JAPAN
Tel./Fax. 03-3953-4633

TOSHIO NOMURA (Japan)
AD, D, I: Toshio Nomura *Illustrator*

院長　PRESIDENT
荒井良治　FUMIHARU ARAI

埼玉県川越市砂新田1-14-11 〒350-1137［高階北小学校前］
TEL&FAX. 0492・48・1181 ←"良い歯 いい歯いちばん!"
1-14-11 Sunashinden, Kawagoe-city, Saitama-pref. 350-1137 Japan

ARAI DENTAL CLINIC (Japan)
AD, D: Mayumi Kawabe DF: Kajitany Design *Dental Clinic*

FIVE REMIX

NISHIAZABU YK BIDG
5F. 10 - 1, NISHIAZABU
2 - CHOME, MINATO-KU
TOKYO 106-0031, JAPAN
T E L. 03·5468·5871
FAX. 03·5468·5872
E-mail.o-five@air.linkclub.or.jp
東京都港区西麻布 2 - 10 - 1
西麻布YKビル5F 〒106-0031
オーファイヴ・リミックス(株)

illustrator
白浜美千代
Shirahama Michiyo

〒180-0003東京都
武蔵野市吉祥寺南町
3-1-24パークハウス103
phone.0422-46-4389
fax.0422-44-9519

103 ParkHouse,
3-1-24 Kichijoji-Minami,
Musashino-shi,
Tokyo 180-0003 JAPAN
phone.(+81)422-46-4389
fax.(+81)422-44-9519

E-mail:turukame@bc.mbn.or.jp

棚瀬伸司
Shinji TANASE
Creative Director
President

**Grandcanyon
Entertainment Inc.**

岐阜市切通4丁目19番3号
〒500 8237
Telephone 058 248 5256
Facsimile 058 248 5257
E-mail geitanase@ma4.justnet.ne.jp

220 East 24th St.5D N.Y.
NY 10010 USA
Telephone 212 685 0348
Facsimile 212 685 8092

O-FIVE REMIX (Japan)
AD, D: Shigeru Kanematsu DF: O-Five Remix
Design Firm

MICHIYO SHIRAHAMA (Japan)
D: Junko Anzai I: Michiyo Shirahama *Illustrator*

GRANDCANYON ENTERTAINMENT INC.(Japan)
CD, AD, D: Shinji Tanase DF: Grandcanyon Entertainment
Inc. *Advertising & Graphic Design Firm*

井上麻美子

〒157 東京都世田谷区
喜多見4-14-12
Phone/Fax 03-3416-6927

**Art Director
Hideki TOGASHI**

東京都港区南麻布 2 - 10 - 9
松山ビル5階 〒106-0047
Matsuyama Bldg 2-10-9 Minamiazabu
Minato-ku Tokyo 106-0047 Japan
telephone.03-5443-0078
facsimile.03-5443-0079

E-mail : togashi@gph.broadnet.or.jp

Yoshiko Wada

MEMBER'S
PLAY CLUB
〒640-8351
和歌山市新内20 サンプラザあろち3F
Telephone
0734-32-9509

MAMIKO INOUE (Japan)
AD: Tetsuji Yamamoto D: Sachiko Terajima
DF: Tetsuji Yamamoto Design Office
Copywriter

PERFORMANCE INC. (Japan)
AD: Hideki Togashi D: Shinobu Tanaka
DF: Performance Inc. *Advertising Production*

PLAY CLUB (Japan)
D: Masanobu Taketomo DF: Roku Design Service
Bar

1,2,3, BODYY COO (Japan)
CD, AD, D: Jisaku Ogawa D: Michika Maseda /
Sumie Fujiyoshi *Design Firm*

HANAKO NAKANO (Hong Kong)
CD: Joycelyn Tsung *Asian Art & Furniture
Company*

HAIRMAKE YIPPEE (Japan)
CD: Kenichi Iwamatsu AD: Yoshihiro Ohya
D: Jun Koba *Beauty Salon*

BAR KURIYA (Japan)
D: Hitoshi Kurosaki DF: Creative Planning *Bar*

564 吹田市岸部中4-1-8
PHONE&FAX 06-388-1973
HANDYPHONE 020-592-7755

KEIKO IKUTA (Japan)
AD, D: Misao Matsumoto DF: Garamond Inc.
Photographer

UZEN (Japan)
D: Yasunori Tetsuka DF: Creative Planning *Bar*

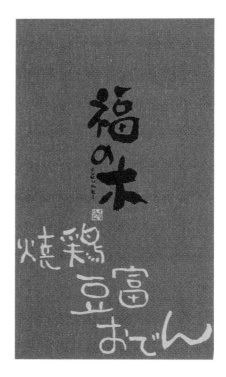

FUKUNOKI (Japan)
D: Hitoshi Kurosaki DF: Creative Planning *Bar*

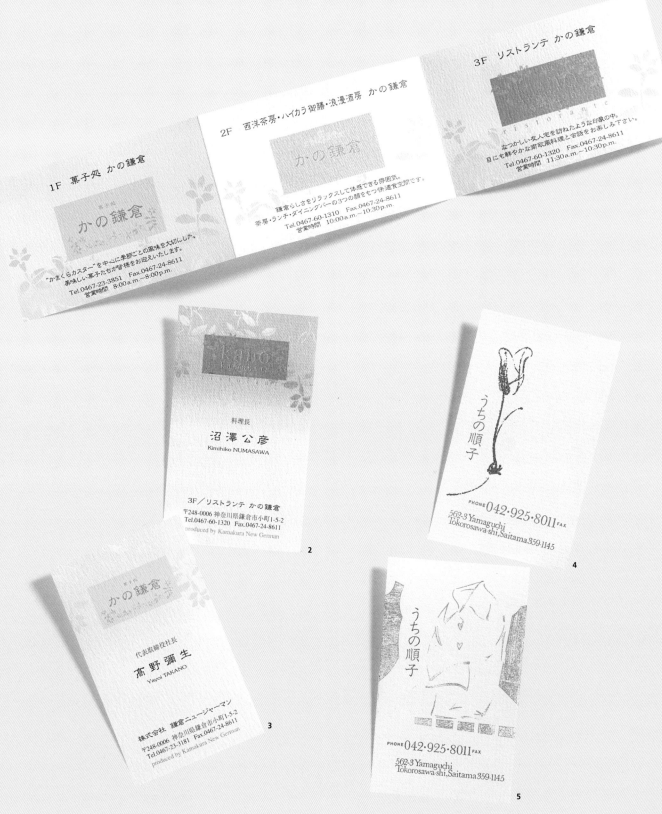

1,2,3, KAMAKURA NEW GERMAN (Japan)
CD: Masahisa Sakamoto AD, D: Koichi Yahata
DF: Hermes Incorporation *Confectionary Maker*

4,5, JUNKO UCHINO (Japan)
AD, D, I: Junko Uchino *Illustrator*

MAD CONCEPT LIMITED (Hong Kong)
AD: Gabriel Tsang D: Iris Kwok DF: Tupos Design Company *Restaurant*

VISAGE CORPORATION (Japan)
AD, D: Mamoru Isobe DF: Visage Corporation
Design Firm

KAZUMI KAGAWA DESIGN OFFICE (Japan)
CD, AD, D: Kazumi Kagawa DF: Kazumi Kagawa
Design Office *Design Firm*

SHAKE IT! (Japan)
CD, AD, D: Fumihiro Yamasaki DF: Yamasaki Design Production Ltd.
Restaurant & Bar

front

NAOKO OGURA PHOTOGRAPHY (Japan)
AD, D: Kay Wakabayashi DF: Kay Wakabayashi Graphic Design
Photographer

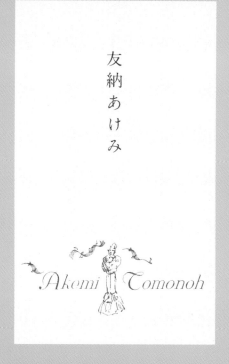

AKEMI TOMONOH (Japan)
AD, D, I: Akihiko Tsukamoto DF: Design Club
Opera Singer

back

NAOKO OGURA PHOTOGRAPHY (Japan)

ETSUKO MURAKAMI (Japan)
D: Kazuhiro Orihara *Artist*

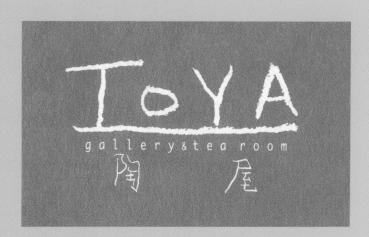

TOYA (Japan)
D: Keisuke Nagatomo D: Mizuki Sakamoto DF: K②
Gallery & Tea Room

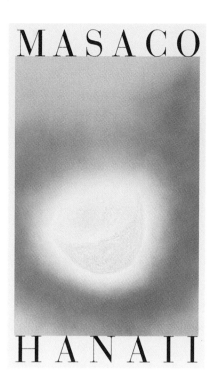

MASACO HANAII (Japan)
I: Masaco Hanaii *Illustrator*

BAR DOGU (Japan)
AD, D: Sachi Sawada DF: "Moss"Design Unit
Bar

BODYY COO (Japan)
CD, AD, D: Jisaku Ogawa D: Sumie Fujiyoshi /
Michika Maseda *Graphic Design Firm*

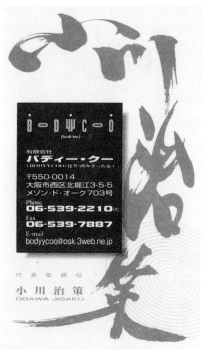

DOMILOGIC (USA)
CD, D, I: Greg Walters DF: Greg Walters Design
Audio & Video Maker

RYUTA YANAGIHARA (Japan)
D: Ryuta Yanagihara *Graphic Designer*

BODYY COO (Japan)

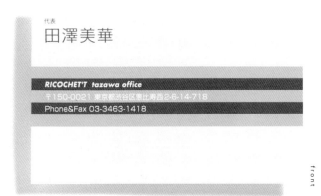

代表
田澤美華

RICOCHET'T tazawa office
〒150-0021 東京都渋谷区恵比寿西2-6-14-718
Phone&Fax 03-3463-1418

front

Mika Tazawa
Exective Producer

*Stylist *Fashion Editor *Writer *Visual Director *Coordinator *Planner
RICOCHET'T tazawa office
#718 2-6-14 Ebisu-nishi Shibuya-ku Tokyo 150-0021 Japan.
Phone&Fax 03-3463-1418

back

TAZAWA OFFICE (Japan)
AD, D: Gen Hosoya DF: Vision Inc. *Stylist*

TAZAWA OFFICE (Japan)

Waffle Panini
Coffee Tea

Waffle'S
beulah
10-3 Daikanyama-cho Shibuya-ku Tokyo 150-0034
TEL: 03-3476-6721 *11:30am-9:00pm (8:30 Last Order)

front

back

WAFFLE'S BEULAH (Japan) CD, AD, D: See Gee Gen DF: Vision Inc. *Coffee Shop*

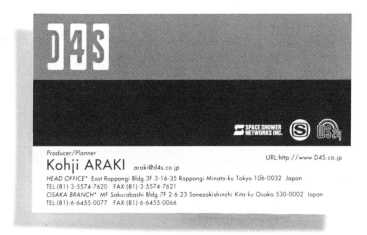

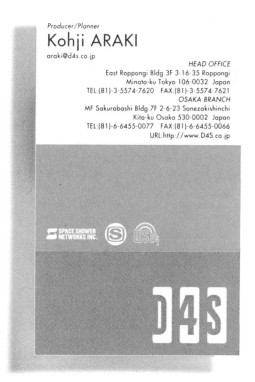

D4S (Japan) AD, D: Gen Hosoya DF: Vision Inc. *Production Company*

55 GRAPHICS (Japan) AD, D: Toshiya Ohyagi / Michihiro Fushikida / Akiko Nakajima DF: 55 GRAPHICS *Graphic Design Firm*

BLUE HEAVEN POOLS (Japan) D: Afei Kitahana *Apparel Maker*

DESIGN NARRATIVE (UK)
CD: Andy Ewan AD: Geniveve Tullberg D, I: Shona McKay
DF: Design Narrative *Design Consultancy*

YUKA MORII (Japan)
AD, I: Yuka Morii D: Teizo Nojima P: Kazunori Yamaji
Clay Artist

TANK GALLERY (Japan)
AD, D: Sachi Sawada DF: "Moss" Design Unit
Cafe & Gallery

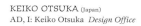

KEIKO OTSUKA (Japan)
AD, I: Keiko Otsuka *Design Office*

FARM YARD BLESSINGS (Australia)
CD, I: Mike Shaw AD, D: Rick Lambert
DF: Rick Lambert Design
Fertilizer

TRICO INTERNATIONAL (Japan)
AD: Hitoshi Saeki DF: Airconditioned *Interior Goods & Furniture Retailer*

MILLENIUM DESIGN GROUP (Canada)
AD: Troy Bailly / Stephen Parkes D: David Papineau
DF: Prototype Design *Website Development Company*

AUSTIN THEATRE FOR YOUTH (USA)
AD, D: Brett Stiles DF: GSD + M *Children's Theatre Company*

JACK TOM DESIGN (USA)
CD, AD, D, I: Jack Tom DF: Jack Tom Design
Design Firm

INDUSTRIAL SOFTWARE TECHNOLOGIES (UK)
CD, AD: Andy Ewan D: Anne Kristin Nybo DF: Design Narrative
Computer Software Company

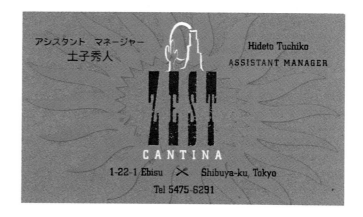

LA BRECQUE CIE. (USA)
CD, AD: Stan Evenson D: Toby Yoo
DF: Evenson Design Group
Consultancy

ZEST CANTINA (Japan)
CD, AD, D: Petrula Vrontikis D: Tammy Kim DF: Vrontikis Design Office
Restaurant

1. KIMIHIKO NAGASE (Japan) AD, D: Masahiro Kakinokihara DF: Draft Co., *Ltd. Artist*
2. ETTA GROTRIAN (Germany) CD, AD, D, I: Gesine Grotrian DF: Gesine Grotrian Design *Historian*
3. NINA NICOLAISEN (Germany) CD, D: Gesine Grotrian AD: Nina Nicolaisen DF: Gesine Grotrian Design *Interior Designer*
4. GESINE GROTRIAN (Germany) CD, AD, D, I: Gesine Grotrian DF: Gesine Grotrian Design *Illustrator*

IDEA PLUS CREATION (Canada)
CD, D, I: Andy Ip DF: Andy Ip Design
Design Firm

CAFÉ DE CELLAR (Canada)
CD, D, I: Andy Ip DF: Andy Ip Design *Cafe*

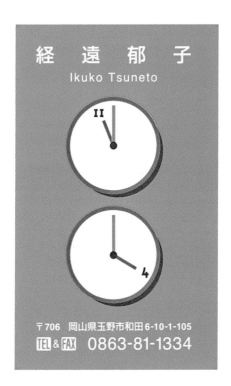

IKUKO TSUNETO (Japan)
D: Ikuko Tsuneto *Graphic Designer*

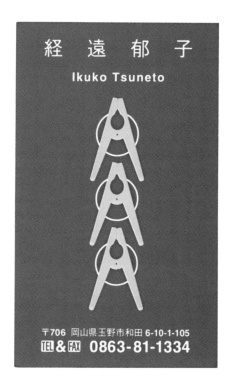

IKUKO TSUNETO (Japan)
D: Ikuko Tsuneto *Graphic Designer*

BRETT STILES (USA)
AD, D: Brett Stiles DF: GSD + M
Designer

1999 IOWA STATE FAIR (USA)
CD, AD, D, I: John Sayles
DF: Sayles Graphic Design
Annual Fair Organizer

1997 IOWA STATE FAIR (USA)
CD, AD, D, I: John Sayles DF: Sayles Graphic Design
Annual Fair Organizer

RACCOON RIVER BREWING COMPANY (USA)
CD, AD, D, I: John Sayles
DF: Sayles Graphic Design *Brew Pub*

ALPHABET SOUP (USA)
CD, AD, D, I: John Sayles DF: Sayles Graphic Design
Toy Store

MANNY'S (USA)
CD, AD, D: Sonia Greteman AD, D: James Strange
DF: Greteman Group *Air & Water Systems Company*

1. TODAYS TRAVELER (USA) CD, AD, D: Rick Eiber DF: Rick Eiber Design (RED) *Travel Agency*
2. JAMI-ART (Poland) CD, AD, D: Tadeusz Piechura CW: Jadwiga & Michal Mrowinscy DF: Atelier Tadeusz Piechura *Graphic Design Firm*

Commercial Vending

Jim Fritzemeier
Vice President

SINCE 1965

front

COMMERCIAL VENDING (USA)
CD, AD: Sonia Greteman AD, D: James Strange
Production Artist: Jo Quillin DF: Greteman Group
Vending Machine Maker

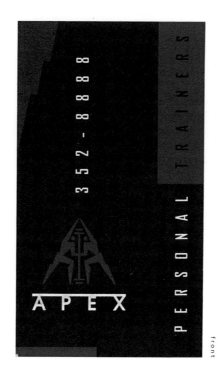

front

APEX (USA)
CD, AD, D: Sonia Greteman AD, D: James Strange
DF: Greteman Group *Personal Trainers*

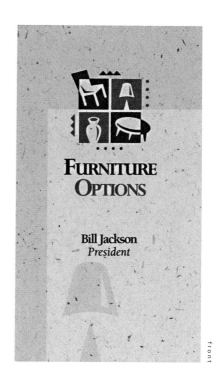

front

FURNITURE OPTIONS (USA)
CD, AD: Sonia Greteman AD, D: James Strange
D: Jo Quillin DF: Greteman Group
Furniture Retailer

back

COMMERCIAL VENDING (USA)

back

APEX (USA)

back

FURNITURE OPTIONS (USA)

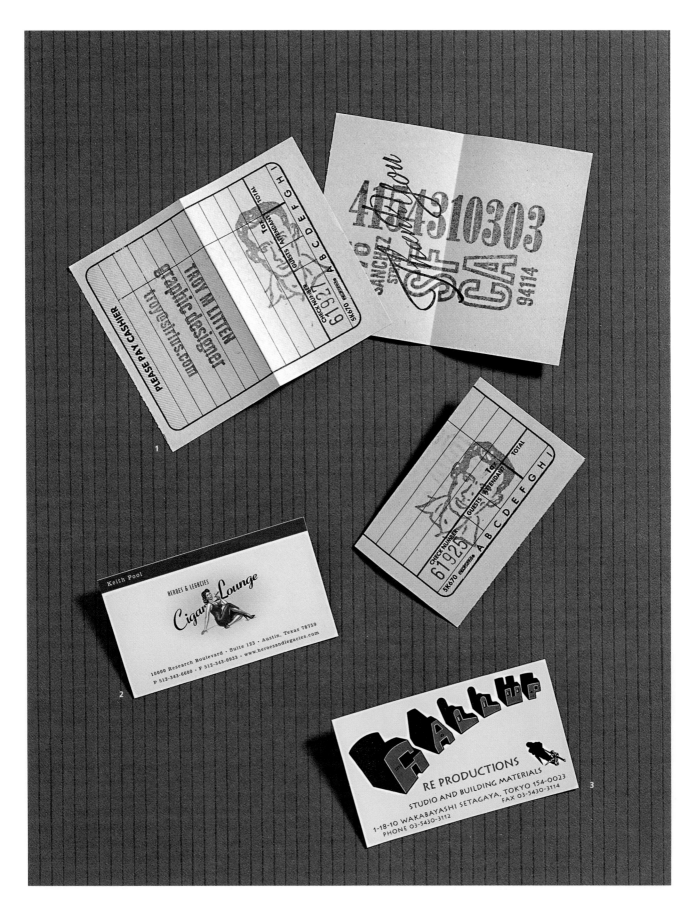

1, TROY M. LITTEN (USA) CD, AD, D, I: Troy M. Litten DF: Troy M. Litten Design *Graphic Designer*
2, HEROES & LEGACIES (USA) AD, D: Brett Stiles I: Mike Griswald DF: GSD + M *Cigar Lounge*
3, GALLUP (Japan) CD: Takeyoshi Naraoka *Interior Goods Retailer*

KEITH BERR PRODUCTIONS, INC. (USA)
CD, D, I: Mark Murphy I: Nirut DF: Murphy Design
Photography Studio

KEITH BERR PRODUCTIONS, INC. (USA)

WRAPIT INC. + 1420 East 31st Street
+ Cleveland + Ohio
+ 44114

216 566 7950 p
216 566 7951 f

wrap it } *photographic coverings for XL applications*

FOOD PAILS AUSTRALIA (Australia)
AD, D: Sophie Bartho DF: Sophie Bartho & Associates
Package Maker

BDMANIA (Portugal)
D: José Rui Fernandes I: Peter Bagge / Mike Allred / Vaugnn Bodé
DF: Duo Design *Comic Book Shop*

DESIGN PUBLICATIONS (USA)
CD, AD, D, I: John Sayles DF: Sayles Graphic Design
Magazine Publisher

DESIGN PUBLICATIONS (USA)

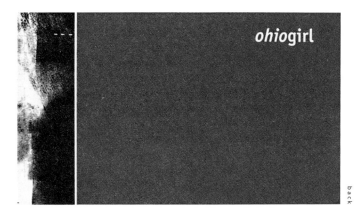

OHIO GIRL (USA)
CD, AD, D: Andy Mueller AD, D: John Fuller DF: Ohio Girl
Design, Film & Photography Studio

OHIO GIRL (USA)

OHIO GIRL (USA)
CD, AD, D: Andy Mueller AD, D: John Fuller DF: Ohio Girl
Design, Film & Photography Studio

NORTH BEACH NOW (USA)
CD, AD: Bruce Yelaska D: Kelly Low
CW: Joan Dahlgren DF: Bruce Yelaska Design
Publisher

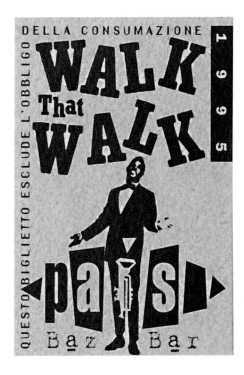

AVANZI SRL (Italy)
D: Jump Gerbella DF: Jump©Gerbella
Disco Bar

CRUSH (USA)
D: Pieter Woudt DF: Big Bolt Graphics *Promoter*

UNIVERSITY OF REGINA BOOKSTORE (Canada)
CD, AD: Catharine Bradbury D: Dean Bartsch DF: Bradbury Design Inc.
University Bookstore

MURPHY DESIGN (USA)
CD, D, I: Mark Murphy DF: Murphy Design *Design Firm*

MURPHY DESIGN (USA)

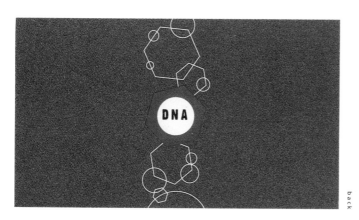

D.N.A. BRAND MECHANICS (USA)

D.N.A. BRAND MECHANICS (USA)
CD, AD, D, I: Lonnie Weis DF: Weis Design *Advertising Agency*

Corporate literature is like a spokesperson for an organisation. That person will not be judged simply on what they say but more on how they say it.

When the visual language of a corporation is pertinent and potent, then its corporate literature offers an engaging exploration of the character attributes and positive values of the organisation.

Good packaging does a lot more than protect the life of the product, it should bring the product to life: firstly by drawing attention to it, then positioning it, and finally adding to and becoming part of its appeal. For packaging to work over and over again, in the home and on the supermarket shelf, it is vital that the visual language expresses the truth of the product.

1. COZZOLINO ELLETT DESIGN D'VISION (Australia) CD, AD, D: Phil Ellett CD: Mimmo Cozzolino I: Jeff Fisher CW: David McIntosh DF: Cozzolino Ellett Design D'Vision
    Design Firm
2. BARRICK ROOFING (USA) CD, AD, D, I: John Sayles DF: Sayles Graphic Design *Roofing Company*
3. BIG DADDY PHOTOGRAPHY (USA) CD, AD, D, I: John Sayles DF: Sayles Graphic Design *Photography Studio*

CONSOLIDATED CORRECTIONAL FOOD SERVICES (USA)
CD, AD, D, I: John Sayles DF: Sayles Graphic Design
Food Service Provider

HILL AVENUE DRUGS (Canada)
CD, AD, D: Catharine Bradbury DF: Bradbury Design Inc. *Pharmacy*

BRAINSTORM (USA)
CD, D: Paula Bee DF: Paula Bee Design *Advertising Company*

ARS MUNDA (Netherlands)
CD, AD, D: Rob Stahl CD, AD, D, I: Annebeth Nies
DF: Stahl Design *Furniture Wholesaler*

ARS MUNDA (Netherlands)

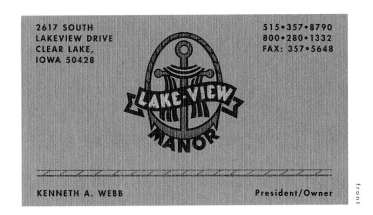

LAKE VIEW MANOR (USA)
CD, AD, D, I: John Sayles DF: Sayles Graphic Design *Hotel*

LAKE VIEW MANOR (USA)

JOHN WIESE (USA)
AD, D, DF: John Wiese *Designer*

KRISTIN KELLY (USA)
CD, AD, D, I: Jeff Fisher DF: Jeff Fisher LogoMotives
Day Care Provider

CUTLER TRAVEL MARKETING (USA)
CD, AD, D, I: John Sayles DF: Sayles Graphic Design
Travel Marketing Company

CUTLER TRAVEL MARKETING (USA)

front

back

DES MOINES PLUMBING (USA)
CD, AD, D, I: John Sayles DF: Sayles Graphic Design *Plumbing Company*

DES MOINES PLUMBING (USA)

ABLE PLUMBING & HEATING (Canada)
CD, AD: Catharine Bradbury D: Dean Bartsch DF: Bradbury Design Inc.
Plumbing Heating Company

R&I PUBLISHERS (Japan)
CD, AD, D: Zempaku Suzuki DF: BBI Studio Inc. *Publishers*

LAZARUS USA (USA)
CD, AD, D, I: John Sayles DF: Sayles Graphic Design
Consultancy

BIG DEAHL (USA)
CD, AD: José A. Serrano D: Jeff Samaripa I: Miguel Perez DF: Mires Design, Inc.
Visual Service Company

1. DOMINIQUE CORBASSON (France) I: Dominique Corbasson *Illustrator*
2,3. FRANÇOIS AVRIL (France) I: Françoirs Avril *Illustrator*
4. CLINIQUE (Netherlands) CD, AD, D: Rob Stahl CD, AD, D, I: Annebeth Nies DF: Stahl Design *Bar & Restaurant*

1, JUDE HUNTLEY (Australia) AD, D, I: Saskia Ericson DF: SAS Art *Jewelry Designer*
2, H. P. DECO (Japan) D: Musubi Aoki *Furniture Retailer*

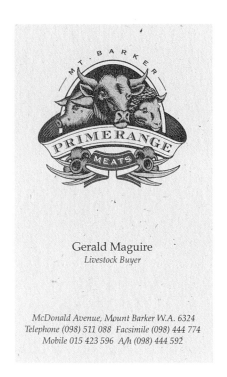

MT BARKER MEATS (Australia)
CD, D, I: Mike Barker AD: Rick Lambert
DF: Rick Lambert Design
Meat Processing & Distribution Company

CINEKINETIC PTY LTD. (Australia)
CD, D: Ben Phillips AD: Rick Lambert DF: Rick
Lambert Design *Camera Equipment Maker*

GOOCH N' ALLIES (USA)
CD, AD, D: Mike Keating DF: Dzine Wise Design
Studio *Pet Goods Shop*

PLANET HAIR (USA)
CD, AD: Sonia Greteman AD: James Strange
D: Garrett Fresh DF: Greteman Group
Beauty Salon

CITY OF WICHITA PUBLIC ART (USA)
CD, AD: Sonia Greteman AD, D: James Strange
DF: Greteman Group *Public Organization*

GOOCH N' ALLIES (USA)

1. GRAN COLOMBIA (USA) CD, AD, D, I: Sonia Greteman D: James Strange / Craig Tomson DF: Greteman Group *Cigar Manufacturer*
2. POLO CLUB (USA) CD, AD: Sonia Greteman AD, D: James Strange Production Artist: Jo Quillin / Garrett Fresh DF: Greteman Group *Polo Club*
3. DIVA (USA) CD, AD, D, I: Jeff Fisher DF: Jeff Fisher LogoMotives *Hair & Nail Salon*

1. FERGUSON FALLS ESTATE (Australia) CD, D, I: Mike Barker AD: Rick Lambert DF: Rick Lambert Design *Winery*
2. RITCHIE ASSOCIATES (USA) CD: Sonia Greteman AD, D: James Strange P: Steve Rasmussen CW: Deanna Harms Finished Art: Todd Gimlin DF: Greteman Group *Architects*
3. ERIC FISHER (USA) CD, AD, D: Sonia Greteman D: Jo Quillin DF: Greteman Group *Beauty Salon*

1. MIYAKO NOMURA (Japan) AD, D, I: Miyako Nomura *Illustrator*
2. VAZARA BASIC (Japan) AD, D: Yoshiro Kajitani D: Mayumi Kawabe P: Ichiro Kamei DF: Kajitany Design *Beauty Salon*
3. JAMBA JUICE (USA) AD, D: Jack Anderson D: Lisa Cerveny / Suzanne Haddon I: Mits Katayama DF: Hornall Anderson Design Works, Inc.
    Fresh Juice & Smoothies Retailer

MIHAELA BELAK (Slovenia) CD, D, I: Jasna Andrić *Ceramic Artist*

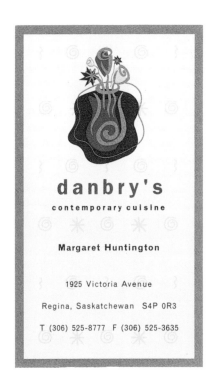

COOK IN THE CLOSET (Australia)
AD: Darren Ledwich D, I: Ross Sabatini
DF: Cozzolino Ellett Design D'Vision
Catering Company

DANBRY'S CONTEMPORARY CUISINE
(Canada) CD, AD, D: Catharine Bradbury
DF: Bradbury Design Inc. *Restaurant*

HOTEL FORT DES MOINES (USA)
CD, AD, D, I: John Sayles
DF: Sayles Graphic Design *Hotel*

FASCHING & FASCHING (Austria) AD, D: Sigi Ramoser D, I: Klaus Österle DF: Atelier für Text und Gestaltung *Photography Studio*

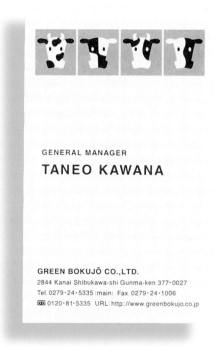

GREEN BOKUJO CO., LTD. (Japan)
CD: Mari Kariya AD, D, I: Yoshiro Kajitani
D: Mayumi Kawabe DF: Kajitany Design
Cattle Ranch

XS MÖBEL FÜR KINDER (Germany)
CD, AD, D, P, I, CW: Oliver A. Krimmel /
Anja Oslerwalder DF: i-d Buero
Children's Furniture Maker

CYNTHIA ROWLEY (Japan) CD, AD, D: Bill Keenan *Apparel Maker*

SNOW CITY CAFE (USA) CD, AD, D, I: Lonnie Weis DF: Weis Design *Restaurant*

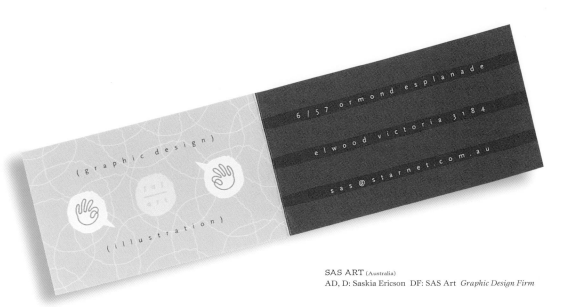

SAS ART (Australia)
AD, D: Saskia Ericson DF: SAS Art *Graphic Design Firm*

SALAMANDRA ESTUDIO (Brazil)
CD, AD, D: Ruth Klotzel I: Edith Derdyk
DF: Estudio Infinito *Music Producer*

M 2 KIKAKU (Japan)
AD: Keisuke Nagatomo D: Shinsuke Yamada
I: Rie Miyazawa DF: K②
Talent Agency

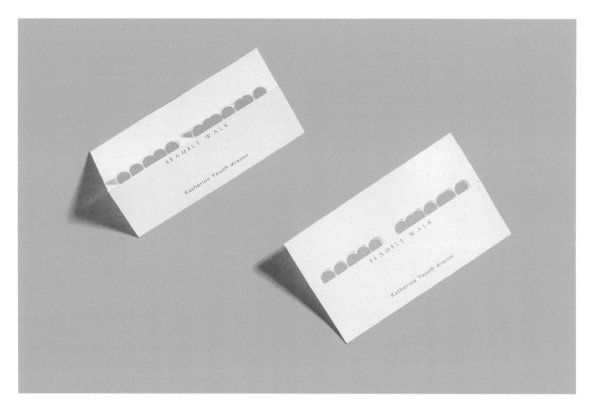

BRAMBLE WALK SDN BHD (Malaysia)
CD: Dharma Somasundram AD, I: Vicky Lee DF: Dentsu Young & Rubicam SDN BHD *Chinaware Retailer*

NIKKI GOLDSTEIN (Australia)
CD, AD, D: Andrew Hoyne P: Marcus Struzina
DF: Hoyne Design *Writer*

INTER ISLAND, INC. (Japan)
AD: Kunio Hayashi D: Yoko Inui
DF: Communication Design Corp.
Editorial Planning Company

GREENPEEL (Switzerland)
CD, AD: Heinz Wild D: Marietta Albinus I: Gavin Patterson
DF: Wild & Frey *Natural Cosmetics Retailer*

1, NÎMES (Japan) CD: M. Design Inc. AD: Michael Tackre I: Miho Matsui / Takahiro Mashiba *Fashion Retailer*
2, BLAUW & WIT (Japan) CD: M. Design Inc. AD: Michael Tackre I: Maiko Nakagawa *Fashion Retailer*
3, LE PETIT BLEU (Japan) CD: M. Design Inc. AD: Michael Tackre I: Takahiro Mashiba *Fashion Retailer*
4, SAKIKO MATAKI (Japan) I: Sakiko Mataki *Illustrator*

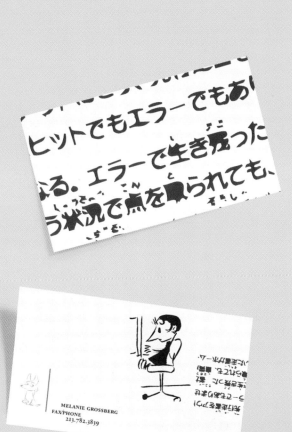

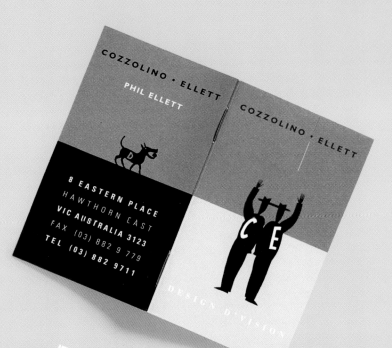

COZZOLINO ELLETT DESIGN D'VISION (Australia)
CD, AD, D: Phil Ellett CD: Mimmo Cozzolino I: Jeff Fisher
CW: Brendan Wright DF: Cozzolino Ellett Design D'Vision
Design Firm

MELANIE GROSSBERG (USA)
AD, D: Melanie Grossberg I: Juan Ortiz DF: Soba Studio
Design & Illustration Studio

HOLLIDAY INN (Netherlands)
CD, AD, D, CW: Rob Stahl CD, AD, D, I: Annebeth Nies
DF: Stahl Design *Hotel Restaurant*

LATIDO (Protugal)
AD, D: Emanuel Barbosa DF: Vestigio
Pet Shop

STUDIO GUARNACCIA (USA)
I: Steven Guarnaccia DF: Studio Guarnaccia
Illutrator

SMILE (Japan)
AD, D: Mika Noguchi DF: Miranda Co. *Copywriter*

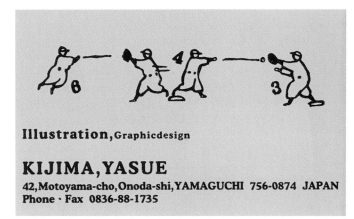

YASUE KIJIMA (Japan)
D, I: Yasue Kijima *Illustrator & Designer*

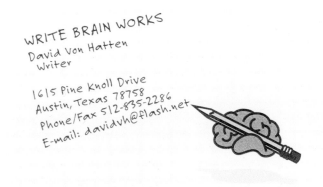

WRITE BRAIN WORKS (USA)
AD, D, I: Brett Stiles DF: GSD + M *Writer*

B5 RECORDS (USA)
CD: John Taylor AD, D: Patty Palazzo DF: T.T.P. Art
Record Label & Recording Studio

front

CACCIATORA (Japan)
AD, D: Hirosuke Ueno *Restaurant*

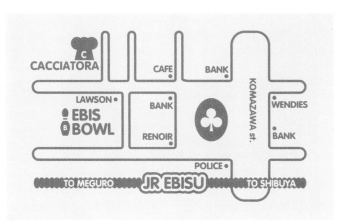

back

CACCIATORA (Japan)

RECYCLART (Belgium)
DF:Signé Lazer *Cultural Organization*

front

AMAZING TWINS DESIGN WORKSHOP LTD.
(Hong Kong) CD, AD, D, I, CW: Benny Au / Colan Ho
DF: Amazing Twins Design Workshop Ltd.
Graphic Designers

MASAHIKO HIRANO (Japan)
CD, AD, D, I: Masahiko Hirano *Advertising Planner*

SWATCH STORE (Japan)
Wristwatch Retailer

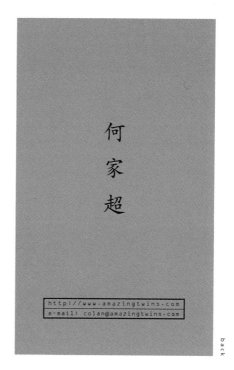

back

AMAZING TWINS DESIGN WORKSHOP LTD.

DENTE DE LEITE (Portugal)
AD, D: Emanuel Barbosa DF: Vestígio
Baby Articles Retailer

SCREAM RACING (USA)
CD, AD, D, I: Michael J. James DF: The Designpond
Racing Company

BRAIN CHILD (USA)
CD, AD, D: Carlos Segura DF: Segura Inc.
Advertissing Agency

THE DOG HOUSE (USA)
CD, AD, D: Clifford Cheng P: Flat Bed Scanner
DF: Voice Design *Snack Shop*

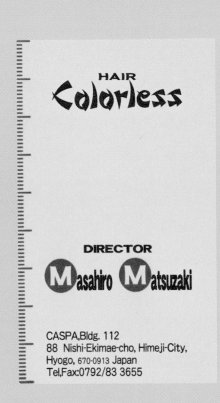

COLORLESS (Japan)
CD, AD, D: Mototaka Sakitani DF: Design Office OO1
Beauty Salon

DANNY FIRST INC. (USA)
CD, AD, D, I: Danny First *Boutique*

BEARHOLIC (Japan)
CD, AD: Takahisa Kamiya *Fashion Goods Retailer*

●東京・代官山店 / 〒150 東京都渋谷区猿楽町12-8　TEL 03-3780-0755 FAX 03-3780-3436
●大阪・近鉄阿倍野店 / 〒545 大阪府大阪市阿倍野区阿倍野筋 1-1-43 近鉄百貨店阿倍野店 8F TEL & FAX 06-625-0031
●大阪・プランタンなんば店 / 〒542 大阪府大阪市中央区千日前 2-10-1 プランタンなんば店 B2F TEL & FAX 06-634-2006
●浜松サゴー店 / 〒430 静岡県浜松市千歳町108 モールプラザサゴー2F TEL & FAX 053-457-3826

GIRL'S MUR MUR (Japan)
CD, AD: Takahisa Kamiya *Fashion Goods Retailer*

Eric Fuchsman
General Manager

212/674-1068
fax 212/674-1825
40 East 20th Street
New York, NY 10003

DESIGN PACIFICA (USA)
CD: Todd Pierce AD, D, I: Jeff Fisher
DF: Jeff Fisher LogoMotives
Design Firm

HULA MOON (Japan)
D: Moon of Japan, Inc. *Fashion Retailer*

PACIFIC FURNITURE SERVICE (Japan)
Interior & Furniture Retailer

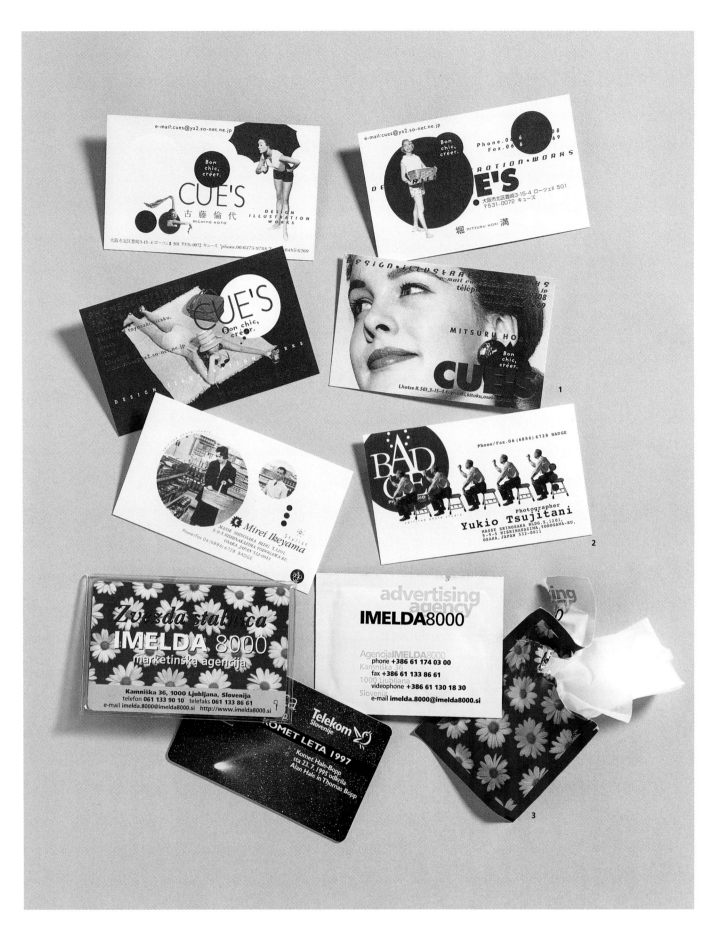

1. CUE'S (Japan) CD, AD, D: Mitsuru Hori DF: CUE'S *Graphic Design Firm*
2. BADGE PHOTO STUDIO (Japan) CD, AD, D: Mitsuru Hori DF: CUE'S *Photography Studio*
3. IMELDA 8000 (Slovenia) CD, AD, D: Jasna Andrič CD, AD: Sašo Urukalo DF: Imelda 8000 *Marketing Agency*

FLAMINGO STUDIO INC. (Japan)
CD, AD, D: Flamingo Studio I: Terry Johnson / TARA
Graphic Design Firm

TAKAKOSTA RODRIGUES (Japan)
CD: Flamingo Studio Inc. *Writer*

MY SHOP CERAMICS (Australia)
AD: Glenn Gould D: Dani Abel
DF: Kajun Design Pty Ltd.
Ceramics Retailer

FLOWERS WITH ESSENCE (Australia)
AD: Glenn Gould D: Dani Abel
DF: Kajun Design Pty Ltd. *Flower Retailer*

KAPUSERU 57 GOU (Japan)
CD, AD: Takahisa Kamiya *Fashion Goods Retailer*

MORE'S INC. (Japan)
AD, D: Hirosuke Ueno *Beauty Salon*

ANIMAL LOVE (Japan)
CD, AD: Takahisa Kamiya *Fashion Goods Retailer*

BEBE'S ANTIQUES (Japan)
AD, D: Hirosuke Ueno *Antique Agency*

POPTUNE TOKYO (Japan)
CD, AD: Takahisa Kamiya *Fashion Goods Retailer*

HIROSUKE UENO (Japan)
AD, D: Hirosuke Ueno *Illustrator & Designer*

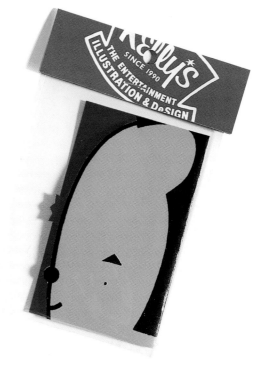

MASAHIRO MATSUBARA (Japan)
D, I: Masahiro Matsubara *Illustrator & Designer*

ICON (Japan)
D, I: Koji Nakata DF: Icon
Illustration & Design Firm

HIROSHI FUJII / HARUO FUJII (Japan)
D, I: Hiroshi Fujii I: Haruo Fujii *Illustrator & Character Designer*

MINORU TAHARA (Japan)

MINORU TAHARA (Japan)
CD, AD, D: Chizuru Sugihara *Construction Company*

GARY'S HOT RODS (USA)
CD, AD, D: José A. Serrano I: Tracy Sabin DF: Mires Design, Inc.
Custom Hot Rod Shop

HOT ROD HELL (USA)
CD, AD, D: José A. Serrano I: Tracy Sabin
DF: Mires Design, Inc. *Custom Hot Rod Shop*

GOODWIN TUCKER GROUP (USA)

GOODWIN TUCKER GROUP (USA)
CD, AD, D, I: John Sayles DF: Sayles Graphic
Design *Restaurant Equipment Distributor*

LARGE HARDWEAR (USA)
D: Sandy Gin DF: Sandy Gin Design
Mountain Bike Clothing Company

*HIGH LANDER (Japan)
CD, AD: Zempaku Suzuki D: Masahiro Naito DF: BBI Studio Inc.
Maintainance Service Company

BAGNO FANTINI (Italy)
D: Jump Gerbella DF: Jump©Gerbella *Beach Bar*

www.media-network.com

Hans Hartman
Execuive Producer

hans@media-network.com
821 Sansome Street
San Francisco, CA 94111
v 415.283.1811 x 1888
f 415.283.1801

MEDIA-NETWORK (USA)
CD, AD, D: Bruce Yelaska DF: Bruce Yelaska Design
Multimedia Company

www.media-network.com

Cloude Porteus
IS Architect

cloude@media-network.com
821 Sansome Street
San Francisco, CA 94111
v 415.283.1811 x 1802
f 415.283.1801

MEDIA-NETWORK (USA)

www.media-network.com

Chris Goldman
Network Systems Analyst

gold@media-network.com
821 Sansome Street
San Francisco, CA 94111
v 415.283.1811 x 2001
f 415.283.1801

MEDIA-NETWORK (USA)

Elly de Lange

Algemene Informatie
010 - 408 11 37

Studieadviseur
Nederlands recht, Fiscaal recht
Telefoon: 010 - 408 15 61
(maandag t/m donderdag)

Erasmus Universiteit Rotterdam. De universiteit die werkt.

ERASMUS UNIVERSITY ROTTERDAM (Netherlands)
CD: Arno Bauman D: Peter Schoonenberg P: Levien Willemse
DF: Studio Bauman BNO *University*

Corine Broeders

Algemene Informatie
010 - 408 11 37

Studieadviseur
Beleid en Management Gezondheidszorg
Telefoon: 010 - 408 85 76
(maandag, dinsdag, donderdag)

Erasmus Universiteit Rotterdam. De universiteit die werkt.

ERASMUS UNIVERSITY ROTTERDAM (Netherlands)
CD: Arno Bauman D: Peter Schoonenberg P: Levien Willemse
DF: Studio Bauman BNO *University*

PUNCTUATION CREATIVE CORP (Malaysia)
CD, AD, D, I: Ping AD: Chris I: Alex DF: Punctuation Creative Corp
Design & Creative Services Company

PUNCTUATION CREATIVE CORP (Malaysia)
CD, AD, D, I: Ping AD: Chris / Jonathan P: Joe Chan,
Hilton Photographers I: Alex DF: Punctuation Creative Corp
Design & Creative Services Company

THE DESIGNPOND (USA) CD, AD, D, I: Michael J. James DF: The Designpond *Design Firm*

index

index

index

new
business
card
graphics 2

Jacket design   Yutaka Ichimura
Designer   Yuka Tamaki
Editor   Maya Kishida
Photographer   Kuniharu Fujimoto
Translator   Pamela Miki
Typesetter   Kenichi Hayakawa
Publisher   Shingo Miyoshi

First edition published in 1999
Publisher P·I·E BOOKS
#301, 4-14-6, Komagome, Toshima-ku,
Tokyo 170-0003 JAPAN

editorial   TEL: 03-3949-5010 FAX: 03-3949-5650
            e-mail: editor@piebooks.com
sales   TEL: 03-3940-8302 FAX: 03-3576-7361
            e-mail: sales@piebooks.com

©1999 by P·I·E BOOKS
ISBN4-89444-117-9 C3070

Printed in Japan

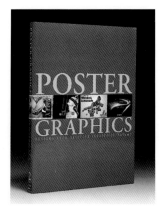

POSTER GRAPHICS Vol.2

Pages: 256 (192 in Color)

700 posters from the top creators in Japan and abroad are showcased in this book - classified by business. This invaluable reference makes it easy to compare design trends among various industries and corporations.

CALENDAR GRAPHICS Vol.2

Pages: 224 (192 in Color)

The second volume of our popular "Calendar Graphics" series features designs from hundreds of 1994 and 1995 calendars from around the world. A rare collection including those on the market as well as exclusive corporate PR calendars.

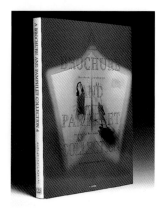

BROCHURE & PAMPHLET COLLECTION Vol.4

Pages: 224 (Full Color)

The fourth volume in our popular "Brochure & Pamphlet" series. Twelve types of businesses are represented through artworks that really sells. This book conveys a sense of what's happening right now in the catalog design scene. A must for all creators.

CATALOG GRAPHICS

Pages: 224 (Full Color)

Here you will find hundreds of practical catalogs and pamphlets, all designed to SELL. Including product descriptions and pictures, prices and options, even order forms, this is an essential collection for anyone seeking ways to stimulate the consumers' desire to buy.

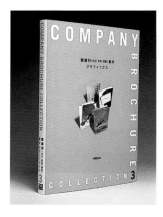

COMPANY BROCHURE COLLECTION Vol.3

Pages: 224 (Full Color)

Company guides and employment manuals from manufacturers, service industries, retailers and distributors; admissions handbooks from universities and professional schools; facilities guides from hotels and sports clubs... Features seldom-seen informational catalogs, categorized by industry.

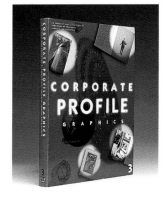

CORPORATE PROFILE GRAPHICS Vol.3

Pages: 224 (Full Color)

The latest catalogs from companies, schools, and facilities around the world. Covers as well as selected inside pages of 200 high-quality catalogs are included, allowing full enjoyment of concepts and layout. Arranged by industry.

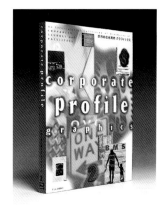

CORPORATE PROFILE GRAPHICS Vol.2

Pages: 224 (Full Color)

The latest volume in our popular "Brochure and Pamphlet Collection" series, featuring 200 carefully selected catalogs from companies around the world. A wide variety, including school brochures, company profiles, and facility guides, is presented.

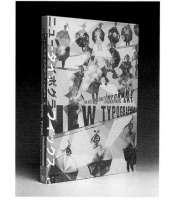

NEW TYPOGRAPHICS Vol.2

Pages: 224 (Full Color)

The latest in international typographic design! Simple, modern design; stimulating visuals; experimental typography; creative yet readable styles... We bring you 400 exhilarating new works from countries that include Germany, Switzerland, the Netherlands, England, America, and Japan.

EVENT FLYER GRAPHICS

Pages: 224 (Full Color)
Here's a special selection zooming in on flyers promoting events. This upbeat selection covers wide-ranging music events, as well as movies, exhibitions and the performing arts.

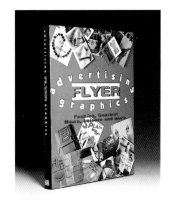

ADVERTISING FLYER GRAPHICS

Pages: 224 (Full Color)

The eye-catching flyers selected for this new collection represent a broad spectrum of businesses, and are presented in a loose classification covering four essential areas of modern life styles: fashion, dining, home and leisure.

TRAVEL & LEISURE GRAPHICS

Pages: 224 (Full Color)

A giant collection of some 400 pamphlets, posters and direct mailings exclusively created for hotels, inns, resort tours and amusement facilities.

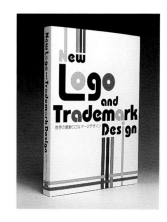

NEW LOGO AND TRADEMARK DESIGN

Pages: 272 (Full Color)

The definitive collection of the latest logomarks from all over the world. With designs ranging from the orthodox to those of audacious young designers, this essential book presents CIs from all types of business, product and event logos, and more. Conveniently arranged by industry.

ONE & TWO COLOR GRAPHICS

Pages: 224 (Full Color)

A giant collection of effective 1 and 2 color designs! Using a minimum number of colors, these designs use eye-catching color combinations, or purposefully subdued colors, to make an impression. These pieces from all corners of the world provide the viewer with strong images and ideas.

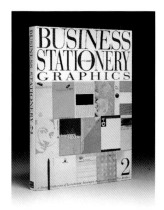

BUSINESS STATIONERY GRAPHICS Vol.2

Pages: 224 (176 in Color)

The second volume in our popular "Business Stationery Graphics" series. This time the focus is on letterheads, envelopes and business cards, all classified by business. This collection will serve artists and business people well.

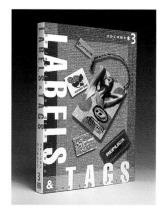

LABELS & TAGS Vol.3

Pages: 216 (Full Color)

From ladies', men's, and unisex fashions, to kids' clothing, jeans, and sports brands, here are more than 1,000 unique labels and tags, classified by item. Expanding the possibilities of fashion graphics, this is the must-have book that designers have been waiting for!

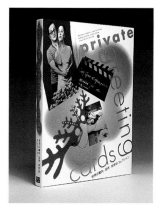

PRIVATE GREETING CARDS

Pages: 224 (Full Color)

A big, new collection of greetings, announcements, and invitations! Christmas, New Year's, and other seasonal cards; birth and moving announcements; invitations to weddings and exhibitions... 450 cards by designers around the world, even more fun just because they're private!

BUSINESS PUBLICATION GRAPHICS Vol.2

Pages: 224 (Full Color)

One volume offering more than 150 samples of regularly published PR and other informative magazines, covering different business sectors from fashion labels to non-profit organizations. This overviews the current trends in PR magazine design purposing to attract the attention of a specific readership in commercial activities.

POSTCARD GRAPHICS Vol.4

Pages: 224 (192 in Color)

Our popular "Postcard Graphics" series has been revamped for "Postcard Graphics Vol.4". This first volume of the new version showcases approximately 1000 pieces ranging from direct mailers to private greeting cards, selected from the best from around the world.

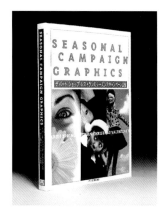

SEASONAL CAMPAIGN GRAPHICS

Pages: 224 (Full Color)

A spirited collection of quality graphics for sales campaigns planned around the four seasons and Christmas, St. Valentine's Day and the Japanese gift-giving seasons, as well as for store openings, anniversaries, and similar events.

SHOPPING BAG GRAPHICS

Pages: 224 (Full Color)

Over 500 samples of the latest and best of the world's shopping bag graphics, from a wide selection of retail businesses! This volume features a selection of the best in shopping bag graphics originating in Tokyo, New York, Los Angeles, London, Paris, Milan and other major cities worldwide, presented here in a useful business classification.

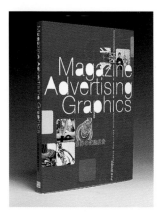

MAGAZINE ADVERTISING GRAPHICS

Pages: 224 (Full Color)

Conceptual, distinctively original magazine ads, selected from 19 countries for their novel, high-impact visuals and attention-grabbing copy (Japanese and English translations provided where copy is essential to the ad's effectiveness). All are model examples of successful promotion production.

PRESENTATION GRAPHICS

Pages: 192 (Full Color)

31 creators from 8 countries illustrate the complete presentation process, from the first idea sketches and color comps, to presentations and the final result. We show you aspects of the design world that you've never seen before in this unique, invaluable book.

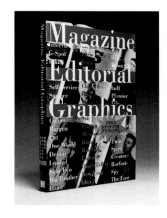

MAGAZINE EDITORIAL GRAPHICS

Pages: 224 (Full Color)

The stylish world of editorial and cover design in a new collection! English avant-garde, French new wave, American energy... 79 hot publications from 9 countries have been selected, all featuring the graphic works of top designers. A veritable New Age design bible.

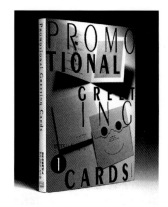

PROMOTIONAL GREETING CARDS

Pages: 224 (Full Color)

A total of 500 examples of cards from designers around the world. A whole spectrum of stylish and inspirational cards, ranging from corporate invitations to private wedding announcements, classified by function for easy reference.

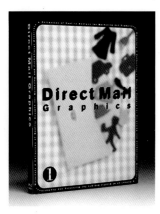

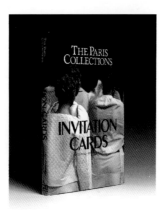

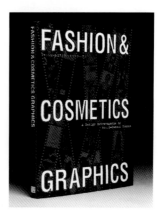

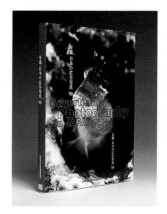

DIRECT MAIL GRAPHICS Vol.1

Pages: 224 (176 in Color)

The long-awaited design collection featuring direct mailers with outstanding sales impact and quality design. 350 of the best pieces, classified into 100 business categories. A veritable textbook of current direct marketing design.

The Paris Collections / INVITATION CARDS

Pages: 176 (Full Color)

This book features 400 announcements for and invitations to the Paris Collections, produced by the world's top fashion brands over the past 10 years. A treasure trove of ideas and pure fun to browse through.

FASHION & COSMETICS GRAPHICS

Pages: 208 (192 in Color)

We have published a collection of graphics from around the world produced for apparel, accessory and cosmetic brands at the vanguard of the fashion industry. A total of about 800 labels, tags, direct mailers, etc., from some 40 brands featured in this book point the way toward future trends in advertising.

ADVERTISING PHOTOGRAPHY IN JAPAN '98

Pages: 224 (Full Color)

Japan's only advertising photography annual! 425 photos selected from talked-about ads of the last four years, these high quality photos stand on their own outside the framework of advertising. The 7th in a series, it was compiled under the supervision of the Japan Advertising Photographers' Association.

CATALOGS and INFORMATION ON NEW PUBLICATIONS

If you would like to receive a free copy of our general catalog or details of our new publications, please fill out the enclosed postcard and return it to us by mail or fax.

CATALOGE und INFORMATIONEN ÜBER NEUE TITLE

Wenn Sie unseren Gesamtkatalog oder Detailinformationen über unsere neuen Titel wünschen.fullen Sie bitte die beigefügte Postkarte aus und schicken Sie sie uns per Post oder Fax.

CATALOGUES ET INFORMATIONS SUR LES NOUVELLES PUBLICATIONS

Si vous désirez recevoir un exemplaire gratuit de notre catalogue généralou des détails sur nos nouvelles publication. veuillez compléter la carte réponse incluse et nous la retourner par courrierou par fax.

P·I·E BOOKS

#301, 4-14-6,komagome, Toshima-ku, Tokyo 170-0003 JAPAN
TEL : 03-3940-8302 FAX : 03-3576-7361